T5-BAL-877

HOW TO PLAY AND TEACH VOLLEYBALL

HOW to PLAY and TEACH VOLLEYBALL

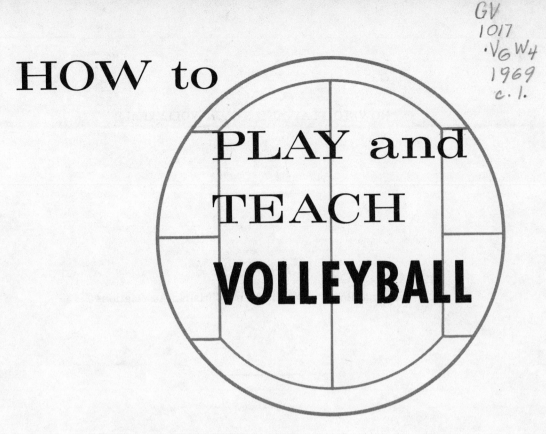

REVISED EDITION

Edited by
J. EDMUND WELCH

Photographs by
LEONARD B. STALLCUP
Official USVBA Photographer

ASSOCIATION PRESS • NEW YORK

HOW TO PLAY AND TEACH VOLLEYBALL

Revised Edition

Standard Book Number: 8096-1727-7

Library of Congress catalog card number: 69-18847

Printed in the United States of America

Contents

			PAGE
	About the Authors		9
	Volleyball—An Olympic Sport		13
	Foreword		15
	Introduction		17
	By Harold T. Friermood		
	"The Spirit of Volleyball"		31
	By Howard G. Danford and J. Edmund Welch		
CHAPTER	1.	Techniques of Serving the Ball	35
		By James C. DeWeese, Jr.	
CHAPTER	2.	Techniques of Passing the Ball	45
		By Murrell Edmunds and J. Edmund Welch	
CHAPTER	3.	Techniques of Setting the Ball	55
		By J. Edmund Welch	
CHAPTER	4.	Techniques of Spiking the Ball	65
		By Marshall L. Walters and Michael F. O'Hara	
CHAPTER	5.	Defense	81
		By William T. Odeneal and J. Edmund Welch	

CHAPTER 6.   Offense   101

>   By William T. Odeneal and J. Edmund Welch

CHAPTER 7.   Requirements and Preparation of Champion
Volleyball Players   113

>   By John C. Lowell and J. Edmund Welch

CHAPTER 8.   Officiating   127

>   By E. Douglas Boyden

CHAPTER 9.   Teaching Techniques   143

>   By Richard C. Nelson

CHAPTER 10.   A Game for Girls and Women   161

>   By Mary Frances Kellam

SELECTED BIBLIOGRAPHY   171

APPENDICES

>   A.   Glossary   179
>   B.   Bulletin Officiel D'Informations   181
>   C.   Hooks' Volleyball Examination   182
>   D.   International Rules Interpretations   187

INDEX   189

ABOUT THE AUTHORS

Dr. Harold T. Friermood retired in 1968 as senior director for health, physical education, and sports, National Council of YMCAs, after serving in this important position for twenty-five years. A member of the distinguished American Academy of Physical Education, former editor of the *Journal of Physical Education,* and past president of the U. S. Volleyball Association, Friermood is recognized as one of America's leading proponents of the sport of volleyball. He spearheaded the American drive to achieve Olympic status for this sport, and he continues to promote the game as a member of the USVBA executive committee and USVBA representative to the U. S. Olympic Committee. Perhaps Friermood's most valuable contribution has been his vital interest in volleyball and in sports in general as a means of furthering ethical behavior and world peace. His efforts in this area will continue in the years ahead.

The late Dr. Howard G. Danford served as athletic director and head of the department of physical education and recreation, Florida State University. He did outstanding work in promoting volleyball among recreation departments, schools, and colleges; and, during his tenure at Florida State University, volleyball was on an equal footing with other sports in the intercollegiate program. He conducted many clinics in the United States and in Europe. Danford died in 1965 while serving as a member of the faculty at Colorado State College, Greeley.

James C. DeWeese, Jr., is general director of the Augusta, Georgia, YMCA. He holds both bachelor's and master's degrees in physical education from Springfield College. At Springfield he played on the varsity volleyball team under the tutelage of Professor Marshall L. Walters. DeWeese learned his volleyball lessons well, as evidenced by his fine work as a volleyball instructor in the YMCA, a coach, a referee, and a promoter of tournaments.

Murrell Edmunds is a New Orleans novelist, playwright, and poet. He is the author of ten published books, some of which have been translated into foreign languages. Few writers have espoused the cause of freedom and human brotherhood with such single-minded devotion and eloquence. Volleyball has been his hobby for over thirty years, during which time he has been one of the most perceptive critics of the game.

Marshall L. Walters is chairman of the department of health, physical education, and recreation, Appalachian State University, Boone, North Carolina. A former professor at Springfield College and metropolitan physical director for the YMCAs of Chicago, Walters has perhaps the longest and most active volleyball career of any of the contributing authors. He is the present editor of *Official Volleyball Guide* and has edited this annual publication for a total of twelve years. He has conducted numerous clinics for the Armed Services in Germany, France, Japan, and Hawaii.

Michael F. O'Hara established a playing record which placed him on the select All-Time Great Volleyball Team. For seven straight years he was chosen as an All-American, and twice during this period he was named the Most Valuable Player of the National Open Championships. He played in the 1959 and 1963 Pan American Games and in the 1964 Olympic Games. O'Hara is now general manager of the Dallas Chaparrals professional basketball team.

Dr. William T. Odeneal is director of athletics at State University of New York, New Paltz. While he was volleyball coach at Florida State University, his teams won three national collegiate championships. Odeneal has conducted clinics for the Armed Forces in Greenland, Newfoundland, Labrador, Hawaii, Spain, Japan, Okinawa, Korea, and Thailand. A prolific writer, his volleyball articles have appeared in many of the physical education and athletic journals. In addition, he is co-author of *Beginning Volleyball* and *Volleyball Syllabus.*

Professor John C. Lowell is director of athletics, Church College of Hawaii, Laie. He is representative of the new leadership in volleyball which helped the U. S. Men's Team win a gold medal at the 1967 Pan American Games. He was manager of that team and also of the U. S. Men's Team in the 1968 Olympic Games. Lowell studied volleyball in Poland in 1966 as a representative of the U. S. State Department. His various articles on international styles of play and conditioning practices have had a pervasive influence on volleyball in North America.

E. Douglas Boyden is the former president of the U.S. Volleyball Association. He is the current chairman of the U. S. Olympic Committee for Men's Volleyball. During the late 1950's, Boyden was chairman of the USVBA officials' and certification committee, and he did much to standardize officiating practices. He has conducted clinics in Hawaii and Japan, and he is co-author of *Staging Successful Tournaments* and *Volleyball Syllabus.* For many years he was a YMCA physical director and executive. At present, he is executive director, United Fund, San Antonio and Bexar County, Texas.

Dr. Richard C. Nelson is associate professor of physical education, The Pennsylvania State University. A frequent contributor to *Research Quarterly,* he works regularly on laboratory studies concerning human performance. One of his studies revealed that a volleyball spike goes 67.7 miles per hour and not 110 miles per hour as so often claimed. Nelson is a former All-American in the Armed Forces Division and in the Collegiate Division, and he has coached volleyball at Michigan State University.

Professor Mary Frances Kellam of the University of North Carolina, Chapel Hill, is active in volleyball in the Division for Girls' and Women's Sports, American Association for Health, Physical Education, and Recreation, and in the U. S. Volleyball Association. She is the DGWS representative to the USVBA and is a member of the U. S. Olympic Committee for Women's Volleyball. She has served on the DGWS national volleyball committee, the DGWS executive council, and the USVBA executive committee. Professor Kellam is a co-author of the second edition of *Beginning Volleyball*.

Dr. J. Edmund Welch served as editor for both the first and second editions of *How to Play and Teach Volleyball*. He was editor of *Official Volleyball Guide* for three years and is a former secretary of the U. S. Olympic Committee for Men's Volleyball. His teaching and promotional experience in volleyball includes seven years as a YMCA physical director and twelve years as a college professor. He has conducted clinics in Alaska, Germany, and France. Welch is the author of seventy-seven published articles, studies, and reports, forty-nine of which are on volleyball. At present he is professor of physical education, West Virginia Institute of Technology, Montgomery.

Of the contributing authors, Friermood, Danford, Walters, Odeneal, Boyden, Kellam, Lowell, and Welch have been recipients of the "Leader in Volleyball" award of the U. S. Volleyball Association.

VOLLEYBALL—AN OLYMPIC SPORT

Now that volleyball is being played in the Olympic Games, it is well that all volleyball leaders, coaches, and players give thought to the guiding ideals of the world's greatest athletic contest. The Modern Olympic Games were revived in 1896 by a Frenchman, Baron Pierre de Coubertin. "Drawing a deep inspiration from the ancient Greek Olympic Games, De Coubertin sought to cut across the lines of intense modern nationalism with an athletic spirit and creed of true sportsmanship that would serve three broad purposes: 'First, to spread physical education and sports around the world; second, to raise the standard of physical achievement; and third, to bring the young people of all continents together in order that links of friendship might be formed to replace the deadly contacts of international war.' "[1]

It is clear from contemplating these purposes and from studying the Olympic Creed that De Coubertin's aim was to further international understanding and world peace. He did not intend for the Olympic Games to be used as a means to produce a master race or nation.

Let us move forward in the true meaning of the Olympic Games.

THE OLYMPIC CREED

"The important thing in the Olympic Games is not winning but taking part. The essential thing in life is not conquering but fighting well."—Baron Pierre de Coubertin, founder of the Modern Olympic Games.

---

[1] "The Lessons of the XIV Olympiad," *Physical Recreation*, I (January-April, 1949), p. 18. Cited in Van Dalen, Deobold B., Mitchell, Elmer D., and Bennett, Bruce L., *A World History of Physical Education* (New York: Prentice-Hall, Inc., 1953), p. 277.

Foreword

"WE are living in an era of rapid change—not in an era of revolution. A revolution is followed by a period of relative stability. We cannot expect such a time of tranquility in our lifetime, for rapid change is the only safe forecast concerning our future. Our welfare will be determined by our ability to adjust to these changes." So spoke President James Harlowe of West Virginia University at a recent college commencement.

Dr. Harlowe was speaking of rapid changes in technology, race relations, and foreign affairs. His words are applicable to the world of sports as well. Many changes have occurred in the sport of volleyball since 1960 when the first edition of *How to Play and Teach Volleyball* was published, thus necessitating a major revision of this book.

The fact that volleyball was first played in the Olympic Games in 1964 has had world-wide repercussions on the game, especially in North America. As a result, Canada adopted the International Rules in their entirety. Radical changes in the rules of the United States Volleyball Association have brought these rules almost in line with the International Rules. Likewise, the International Volleyball Federation made some modifications in the International Rules along certain features of the USVBA Rules. The Division for Girls' and Women's Sports, American Association for Health, Physical Education, and Recreation, is considering at the present time changes in their rules to bring them further in line with those of the USVBA.

All of these changes are affecting playing techniques and strategies. Of the number of changes, certainly the most profound for those of us in the United States has been the adoption by our leading teams of international styles of play. The "dink" spike, over-the-net blocking, the "Jap" roll, the three-spiker attack, and the "dive and save" in defensive play make top-flight volleyball a truly different game than it was a decade ago.

The new edition of *How to Play and Teach Volleyball* takes into consideration these new techniques and strategies. As in the first edition, volleyball is presented as played by champions because champions in any sport give us the best picture of how a game should be played. For this reason, *How to Play and Teach Volleyball* will have value to all instructors, coaches, players, officials, and students of the game.

Change in itself, however, does not denote progress. I view two of these

15

changes in volleyball with concern. The first, by far the more important, has to do with the de-emphasis among champions on the Honor Call, a unique contribution by American players and leaders. The second has to do with the substitution of the double forearm pass for the traditional overhand pass in service receptions. This technique distorts a basic concept inherent in the rules of the International Volleyball Federation, the United States Volleyball Association, and the Division for Girls' and Women's Sports of the AAHPER. As editor of this book, I have purposefully stressed the Honor Call and the overhand pass, and I do so without apologies.

All of the contributing authors are highly experienced leaders in the game of volleyball. While group authorship combines the wide experience of many leaders in a field, it does result in different and sometimes opposing viewpoints. In volleyball this is not undesirable, because there are several acceptable ways to play and to teach the game. The reader will notice varying ideas expressed by the authors.

I want to express my appreciation to the contributing authors, who did such an excellent job. In addition, I am grateful to the contributing authors of the first edition who chose not to write for the second edition. These include Roger G. Burton, George J. Creswell, Jr., John K. Clark, and Warren W. Smith. Without their original works, the second edition of *How to Play and Teach Volleyball* would never have materialized.

I am especially indebted to Dr. Thomas E. McDonough, Sr., director emeritus of physical education, Emory University, whose co-operation made the first edition possible; to Harry E. Wilson, editor of the *International Volleyball Review;* to Dr. Leonard B. Stallcup, official USVBA photographer, who made the photographs for this book; and to the late Ernest W. Knabe, who shared with me on many occasions his long experience in volleyball.

Others who furnished technical information for this book include: Professor James E. Coleman, Allen E. Scates, G. R. McDonald, Anton H. Furlani, Professor Don Shondell, Gene O. Chambliss, Wilbur H. Peck, Robert A. Rule, Harlan Cohen, Glen Davies, Hoadley Hagen, Dr. Edgar W. Hooks, Jr., Ken Dunlap, Mark Watson, Jan Prsala, Val Keller, Dr. Richard B. Morland, Catalino R. Ignatio, John L. Griffith, Peter R. Wardale, Vladimir Savvin, C. L. Bobb Miller, Sol H. Marshall, Professor Carl M. McGown, Horace "Smitty" Duke, Jerre McManama, Harold O. Zimman, E. B. DeGroot, Jr., Betty Ann Ghormley, Ida C. Litschauer, Eugene Selznick, Dr. George Pearson, Wez Bridle, Professor Emil Hrenchuk, Martin J. Feely, and Donald Smyth.

The greatest amount of appreciation is due my wife and partner, Edith, who typed and proofed the manuscript and gave me constant encouragement during the long period of this project.

J. Edmund Welch

Department of Physical Education
West Virginia Institute of Technology
Montgomery, West Virginia

Introduction

By HAROLD T. FRIERMOOD

EACH reader of this book will approach and use it in his own particular way. He may want to find out what the editor has in mind and what the members of this carefully chosen panel say about their major topics. If the reader is not familiar with some, or all, of the writers, he may take a look at the editor's comments "About the Authors." A quick check on the "Contents" may spot a particular chapter title that has immediate appeal. A glance through the "Glossary" can be used to up-date one's understanding of terms (noting distinctions made in "passing," "setting," "defense."). The eyes of some readers will be opened when they note the developments in the "Game for Girls and Women." A plan for productive exploration and systematic study may be started by checking the "Selected Bibliography."

Some readers may invite colleagues and staff members to examine and share comments about the book's contributions in such areas as: progress in the game's development since the first edition of this book was published in 1960; how the game has been affected because of its inclusion in the official program of Olympic Games; emphases made in modern teaching concepts; the preparation of players and teams for competition; identification of problems involved in helping players, teachers, recreation leaders, coaches, and officials develop a point of view and practices that will insure desirable outcomes from the game—to the participants, to the sponsoring organizations or institutions, and to the sport itself.

Teachers and coaches may ask pupils and players to study specific sections of the book to insure a common background and understanding of acceptable procedures. Volleyball officials may secure new insights about their responsibilities as they examine the specific chapter describing the qualifications and standards they must meet.

Whatever the methods used by a particular reader in making effective use of this book, it is hoped that a new appreciation will be gained for this USA originated game, one of the newest Olympic sports.

Volleyball and the Modern Olympic Games were launched on successive years; volleyball came first. It was originated in 1895 by William G. Morgan, YMCA physical director in Holyoke, Massachusetts, as a recreational sport. The modern era of the Olympic Games began in 1896 with the first program financed and conducted by the city of Athens. Greece was selected because it had been the site of the ancient games. Held every four years from 776 B.C. until 394 A.D., in the valley of Olympia, the original games had been a sports contest along with cultural programs and pagan religious ceremonies. Following the 1170 years of Games activity an imperial Roman decree terminated the observance. For 14 centuries there was an Olympic void. The idea for rebirth of the Games was nurtured and brought into fruition by a Frenchman, Baron Pierre de Coubertin. Although a young man (only 34 when the Games were revived) he thought deeply, traveled widely, and promoted vigorously the idea that youth, education, and sports belonged together. He believed that encouragement could be given to individual achievement, cultural development, and international understanding by planning and holding a great world-wide quadrennial sports festival of youth. Although the World Alliance of YMCAs was recognized in 1928 by the International Olympic Committee for contributions to world youth through its program of sports, physical education, camping and other character building activities, it was not until 1957 that the IOC approved volleyball as an Olympic sport and seven years later included it on the Games program in Tokyo. But, during the years between the invention of volleyball and its appearance as an Olympic sport, many things of interest happened. A few are presented here.

As a young college graduate William G. Morgan spent his first year in the Auburn, Maine, YMCA and during the summer of 1895 moved to Holyoke, Massachusetts.[1] He took charge of the physical department of the YMCA and as the program was promoted the classes for business men became large—the members enthusiastic.[2] In addition to directed exercise he found some type of recreation and competition was needed. The newly developed game of basketball (the creation of James Naismith at YMCA Springfield College in 1891) seemed suited to the younger men, but there was need for something not quite so rough and strenuous for older members. At this time he had no knowledge of any game similar to volleyball to guide him, and he drew upon his own sports training and practical experiences in the YMCA gymnasium. Describing his early explorations Morgan said,[3]

"In looking for a suitable game, tennis occurred to me, but that required rackets, balls, net, and other equipment, so that was discarded, but the idea of using the net seemed to hold; we raised it to about six feet six inches from the floor, just above the average man's head. We had to have a ball, and among those we tried was the bladder of a basketball, but that proved to be too light and slow; then we tried a basketball, which was too large and too heavy.

"Finally we decided that a ball made on the lines of the present (1916) volleyball was about what we needed and we asked A. G. Spalding & Bros. to make us a ball, which they did (at their nearby factory at Chicopee, Massachusetts). This gave satisfaction. (It was leather covered, with a rubber bladder. The ball was not less than 25 nor more than 27 inches in circumference and weighed not less than nine nor more than 12 ounces)."

Morgan credits a Holyoke physician, Dr. Frank Wood, and the Chief of the Fire Department, John Lynch, both members of his gymnasium classes, with helpful suggestions in developing the initial 10 rules and basic concepts of the game. The original idea of a net between the opposing teams was retained.

Early in 1896 a YMCA physical directors' conference was scheduled at Springfield College. Dr. Luther Halsey Gulick, director of the professional physical education training school (and also executive director of the physical education department, International Committee of YMCAs) invited Morgan to put on an exhibition of the game in the new college gymnasium. Chartering a trolley car, Morgan took two five-man teams and loyal supporters to Springfield where the exhibition was staged before the conference delegates in the East gymnasium. Captain of one team was Mayor J. J. Curran, and, of the other, Fire Chief John Lynch.

Morgan explained that the new game, then called "Mintonette," was designed for the gymnasium or exercise hall but might also be played out-of-doors. Any number of persons could play—the object being to keep a ball in motion over a high net, from one side to the other, played in innings, combining aspects of two games, tennis and handball. After watching the demonstration and hearing Morgan's report, Professor Alfred T. Halstead pointed out the batting or volleying phase of the activity and proposed the name of "Volley Ball." This name was accepted by Morgan and the Conference group. (The name has continued throughout the years with only one slight change: in 1952 the USVBA board of directors voted to spell the name as one word "Volleyball.")

Morgan explained the rules he had worked out, then turned over his hand written copy to the YMCA physical directors' conference as a guide in the use and continuing development of the game. A committee was appointed to study the rules and to devise promotional and teaching suggestions. A brief report about the new game and the rules appeared in the July 1896 issue of *Physical Education*[4] and was included in the 1897 issue of the first OFFICIAL HANDBOOK of the Athletic League of the Young Men's Christian Associations of North America. (The League had been formed the year before.) The rules continued to appear in the *Handbook* until 1916 when the YMCA invited the National Collegiate Athletic Association (NCAA) to join in sponsoring the Spalding Athletic Library blue cover series *Official (Guide* and) *Volley Ball Rules,* published by the

American Sports Publishing Company. The YMCA and other groups continued this sponsorship until 1928.

YMCA physical directors, trained principally in two professional physical education schools: Springfield College in Massachusetts and George Williams College of Chicago (now located in Downers Grove, Illinois), took volleyball to communities throughout the United States and Canada and to many other countries. (Elwood S. Brown—to the Philippines, J. Howard Crocker—China, Franklin H. Brown—Japan, Dr. J. H. Gray—Burma, China, and India; and other early leaders to Mexico, South American, European, and African countries.) Elwood Brown, going to the Philippines in 1910, helped organize and conduct the first Far Eastern Games in Manila in 1913 with volleyball included.

An indication of the growth of the game in the United States is suggested by an article in the 1916 Spalding *Volleyball Guide* by Robert C. Cubbon. Listing players by groups he estimated the number of players to be: YMCA (young men, boys, older men) 70,000; YWCA (ladies and girls) 25,000; playgrounds and recreation departments (boys and girls) 50,000; schools (boys and girls) 25,000; colleges (young men) 10,000; total—200,000 persons.

During World War I, Dr. George J. Fisher, as Secretary of the War Work Bureau of the YMCAs, made volleyball a part of the recreative program in military training camps, at home and abroad. Rules for volleyball were included in the three editions of the Athletic Handbooks prepared for sports and recreation leaders in the Army and Navy. Thousands of balls and nets were shipped abroad for USA troops and some were also presented to sports leaders in the Allied Armies. More than 16,000 volleyballs were distributed in 1919 to the American Expeditionary Forces alone.

In June of 1919 the Inter-Allied Games were held in Paris (but volleyball was not included because it had not yet become sufficiently familiar to all of the 18 participating allied countries to provide balanced and equitable competition).

The 1922 *Guide*[5] had as sponsoring organizations: YMCA, NCAA, Boy Scouts of America, and the Playground Association of America. (The first national volleyball championships in the U.S. were conducted at Brooklyn Central YMCA in 1922. From eleven states and Canada, twenty-three strong YMCA teams participated—Pittsburgh took first and Germantown, Pennsylvania was second.) Additional sponsors for the *Guide* were invited:

1923. National Amateur Athletic Federation.

1924. U.S. Army, U.S. Navy, industrial organizations, Women's division of the National Amateur Athletic Federation. (In this 1924-25 *Guide*, a hope and expectation was projected that volleyball would be recognized by the International Olympic Committee—soon.)

1925-26. Representative of the high schools; a group called Playground and Recreation Association of America (later it became the National Recreation Association and is now known as the National Recreation and Park Association).

1926-27. (*Guide* shifted from "Blue" to Spalding "Red" series; special rules included for women and girls).

1927-28. (A recommendation was announced to make the seventh national YMCA championship an "open" event—with a rotating trophy provided by Herbert L. Pratt; and a "Veterans" championship for players over 35 years of age, to be started—with a rotating trophy provided by the Chattanooga Chamber of Commerce.)

1928. Following the Chattanooga championships (YMCA "Open" won by Germantown, Pennsylvania, with Chicago Hyde Park the runner-up; Veterans tourney won by Chattanooga with Atlanta runner-up), plans were discussed and the organization completed for the United States Volleyball Association on July 9, 1928, in New York City. The previously named organizations and the Young Women's Christian Association were the national groups that launched the USVBA. Dr. George J. Fisher was elected President and Dr. John Brown, Jr., Secretary-Treasurer.

FOUR DECADES OF VOLLEYBALL WITH USVBA SPONSORSHIP

Within the framework of the USVBA, brief highlights about the development and growth of volleyball, from 1928 to the present, follow.

First Decade—to 1938

Although the member groups placed much emphasis upon the instructional and recreational aspects of the game, the USVBA gave attention to these five phases: 1) Annual meeting: to hear about agency plans and activities and to conduct its business, 2) developing rules and standards and issuing the annual *Guide*, 3) the national championship, 4) interpretation and promotion of the game, and 5) seeking out additional national groups as members. Until 1946 the annual meeting was held in New York City several weeks after the tournament. This made it possible to deal quite objectively with the game in its many phases, but did not involve many of the persons who were chiefly concerned as players, teachers, coaches, and officials.

The 1929 national championships were held May 10-11 in Chicago by the Hyde Park Department YMCA at the University of Chicago Bartlett Gymnasium. Amos Alonzo Stagg, the Athletic Director, was an interested spectator. He had been a student at Springfield College nearly 40 years before.

In 1932 the USVBA was made up of: YMCA, NCAA, National Recreation Association, Boy Scouts of America, industrial organizations, National Amateur Athletic Federation, high schools, U.S. Army, U.S. Navy, YWCA, Women's Section of the American Physical Education Association, National

Jewish Welfare Board, Boys' Club Federation, and Camp Fire Girls. Regions were defined and representatives appointed in each. Dr. John Brown, Jr. was named official rules interpreter.

1933. First textbook on men's volleyball, by Robert E. Laveaga, was published by A.S. Barnes & Co. (Women's publication was already available.)

1934. National volleyball referees were recognized and approved.

1935. Six regions designated. Three organizations voted into membership: American Physical Education Association, American Turners, and Amateur Athletic Union. YMCA men active in the AAU, encouraged it to take up volleyball, and served on its volleyball committee, helping to organize tournaments; 1935 event held in San Diego, Calif.

1936-37. One of the members, APEA, changed its name to American Association for Health, Physical Education, and Recreation (AAHPER).

1937-38. Negotiated with AAU to give up its claim of jurisdiction over volleyball. At AAU national convention in Boston, October, 1937, action was taken recognizing the United States Volleyball Association as the official body in the USA and, as such, the proper body to carry on international volleyball affairs.

Tenth anniversary meeting of the USVBA held June 10, 1938.

Second Decade—to 1948

Beginning in 1939 representatives of volleyball players were appointed each year to serve on the USVBA Board.

1940. National Federation of State High School Athletic Associations, general representation from AAHPER, and Federal Housing Authority added to membership of USVBA. Two college teams entered the national championship held in Philadelphia: Temple University and University of Pennsylvania; open tournament won by Los Angeles Athletic Club (first time won by other than a YMCA team).

Country divided into 12 regions in 1942 with USVBA representatives in each. New constitution adopted. Canadian (Ontario) Volleyball Association invited to attend annual meeting on a fraternal basis. At its request, YWCA was discontinued as a member of USVBA at start of 1942 season. Letter from Russian ambassador in Washington, D.C., requesting information about volleyball and copy of U.S. rules. A.S. Barnes & Co. selected as publisher of *Annual Guide and USVBA Rules*. Editor and Business Manager of *Volleyball Review*, Harry E. Wilson and Dr. David T. Gordon, respectively, commended.

William G. Morgan, inventor of volleyball, passed away December 12, 1942.

1943. Volleyball included in the Armed Forces fitness and recreation program. Women published rules in a separate guide—National Section on Women's Athletics of the AAHPER. Dr. Harold T. Friermood succeeded

Dr. John Brown, Jr. as Secretary-Treasurer of USVBA. Last prewar championship held in Minneapolis.

1944. No national tournaments held. May 1 to 7 designated as "National Volleyball Week." Emphasis placed upon wide participation. *Guide* contained full information on stay-at-home "National Volleyball Skills Tournament" for recognition of individual and team points. The 1944 *Guide* listed the national tournament champions from 1922 to 1942, compiled by Andrew A. Hammersmith of Massillon, Ohio.

1945. National Volleyball Week, March 17-24; second National Volleyball Skills Tournament conducted on a wartime stay-at-home basis. Because of the large quantity of *Guides* purchased by the Armed Forces, sales as of June 1, 1945, totaled 39,712.

1946. The instructional, two reel, 16 mm. sound film, "Play Volleyball," was produced at a cost of $7,500 by Association Films, Inc. Following World War II national tournaments resumed in Chicago with annual meetings held in conjunction with the tournaments for the first time. Awards initiated for distinguished service; "Leader in Volleyball" citations and certificates given to Dr. George J. Fisher, C. C. Robbins, A. Provost Idell, Harry A. Batchelor, F. G. McGill, Albert V. Walker, and, posthumously, to Andrew Stewart. Avery Brundage invited to advise on steps needed to have volleyball recognized as an Olympic sport. (USVBA applied for and was soon accepted for membership in the U.S. Olympic Association.) The 1946 *Guide* listed winners of three major trophies: "Robbins"—1923 to 1942, "Chattanooga"—1928 to 1942, and "USVBA-Herbert L. Pratt"—1929 to 1942. (USVBA trophy provided by Thomas J. Watson in 1946.)

1947. This year's *Guide* took account of Golden Jubilee of volleyball (1895-1945). Regions restudied. Revised Constitution and By-Laws reviewed during annual meeting in Houston, Texas. Mexico participated in the national tournament. A mid-year meeting scheduled for the first time to handle the increasing work of the USVBA. Authorized Major E. B. De-Groot, Jr. and Royal L. Thomas as USA official delegates to the International Volleyball Congress in Paris where the International Volleyball Federation (FIVB) was formed early in the year. (USVBA one of 13 original charter members of FIVB.)

1948. Twentieth USVBA anniversary meeting held in South Bend, Indiana. Plan started of volleyball players electing their own representatives to serve on the USVBA Board of Directors (rather than having them appointed as had been done since 1939). USA team made good-will tour of Europe. Direct contacts were made in London by Friermood with IOC members regarding the inclusion of volleyball on the Olympic Games program.

Third Decade—to 1958

1949. "Time game" written into the USVBA rules. Women's and Collegiate divisions added to national tournaments held at Los Angeles. First

Men's World Championships conducted, Prague, Czechoslovakia: 1st-USSR, 2nd-Czechoslovakia. French Consulate in Los Angeles recognized USVBA as one of the charter members of FIVB.

1950. Dr. Fisher retired and Professor Marshall L. Walters was appointed as editor of the annual *Guide*. Printer in Berne, Indiana selected to publish the *Guide*. Authorized and financed a USVBA digest, edited by E. B. DeGroot, Jr., of a world-wide study of volleyball (made and written as a doctoral dissertation at Teachers College, Columbia University by Miss Lu, Hui-Ching). Procedure and point system to use in selecting and recognizing USVBA All-American players approved at Knoxville meeting. National tournament winners chart, prepared by Friermood, shown in 1950 *Guide* expanded to include: U.S. Open, National YMCA, YMCA Veterans, AAU, Turners, Collegiate and Women's events.

1951. Slide film, "Beginning Volleyball" produced and distributed by the Athletic Institute as a tool to extend interest in schools and colleges; Robert E. Laveaga served as the technical expert consultant from the USVBA. Merton H. Kennedy elected Secretary-Treasurer upon the withdrawal of Friermood. Colonel DeGroot, Jr. reported on a study of the USVBA structure and organization. A USVBA citation given to Springfield College (site of the 1951 meetings and tournaments) for its contributions made to the game over the years.

1952. Dr. Harold T. Friermood elected President of the USVBA upon the retirement of Dr. George J. Fisher; vice-presidents: Col. E. B. DeGroot, Jr., A. P. Idell, and Viggo O. Nelson; Secretary-Treasurer, Robert Morrison. During the annual meeting in Columbus, Ohio, a consultation was held dealing with co-ed and women's and girls' volleyball. Masaichi Nishikawa, President of the Japanese Volleyball Association, discussed the Far Eastern style of play with the USVBA Executive Committee. The Physical Education Society of the YMCAs of North America was added to the membership. The USVBA Board of Directors voted to spell the name as one word "Volleyball." An Armed Forces division was added to the tournaments. Further contacts made with IOC during the Olympic Games in Helsinki. World Volleyball Championships held in Moscow: second time for men, first time for women; no USA representatives present.

1953. Observed 25th birthday of USVBA during the annual meeting in Omaha, Nebraska. Logan C. Mundt appointed Editor of the *Guide*. Team from Waseda University, Tokyo, Japan, visited the United States and participated in the national tournament. USA team made a second goodwill tour of Europe. New book, *Modern Volleyball,* by Curtis Ray Emery, published by the Macmillan Co., New York.

1954. During annual meeting in Tucson, Arizona: Committee named, Dr. W. P. Burroughs, chairman, to work with the USOC in the selection and financing of men's and women's teams for 1955 Pan American Games; USVBA working with Helm's Athletic Foundation, set up Volleyball Hall of Fame (named these persons to be recognized: Dr. George J. Fisher, William G. Morgan, A. P. Idell, and James Wortham); approved a project, completed by Edward P. Lauten, of codifying the volleyball playing rules; emphasized the need for the USVBA to adopt a formal written policy dealing with non-discrimination in national championships as discussed the past two years (actual practice had been in accordance with the YMCA written policy, established for all its national sports programs in the fall of 1946). "Leader-in-Volleyball" recognition made to James E. Rogers before Society of State Directors for Health, Physical Education, and Recreation; later the Society applied and was received into USVBA membership. Eighth mid-year meeting held in New York City, November 12, 1954.

1955. Volleyball on the Pan American Games program in Mexico City, March 12-26 (U.S. Men's team first and Women's team second in their respective divisions). Twenty-seventh annual meeting of USVBA held in Oklahoma City. Viggo O. Nelson succeeded Friermood as President. Tournament souvenir program prepared that included an article, "Sixty Years of Volleyball," by Friermood.

1956. The Seattle, Washington, tournaments attended by teams from Hawaii. World Championships held in Paris; two USA teams participated: USA Men—sixth, USA Women—eleventh. Friermood carried on negotiations in Melbourne, Australia, with IOC members, and, on a trip around the world, with leaders in other countries in behalf of Olympic recognition of volleyball.

1957. Volleyball designated an Olympic sport at IOC meeting in fall at Sophia, Bulgaria. Book by E. Douglas Boyden and Roger G. Burton, *Staging Successful Tournaments,* published by Association Press, used to set up national championships.

1958. Thirtieth USVBA anniversary meeting held in Scranton, Pennsylvania. Official score sheet was created and a plan for certifying volleyball scorers and timers was approved. Plans completed for selecting Pan American Games Men's and Women's teams. Completing five issues, Logan C. Mundt was succeeded by Dr. J. Edmund Welch as Editor of the *Annual Reference Guide.* Welch produced the 1959-60-61 editions. American Latvian Association accepted into USVBA membership.

Fourth Decade—to 1968

1959. Annual meeting and national tournaments were held in Des Moines, Iowa. Pan American Games conducted in Chicago: USA Men's team first, USA Women's team placed second in its division (Brazil the winner). After being passively related to the USVBA for 31 years, the Boy Scouts of America discontinued its affiliation. Name of Women's Section on Athletics of AAHPER was changed to Division of Girls' and Women's Sports.

1960. World championships held in Brazil; fourth time for men: winner—USSR, second—Czechoslovakia (USA—sixth); third time for women: winner—USSR, second—Japan (USA—sixth). Annual meeting in Dallas,

Texas. U.S. Marines recommended representatives to serve on USVBA Board. Honor call by a tournament player was picked up by press and featured as something "special" in the game of volleyball. Book, *How To Play and Teach Volleyball,* edited by J. Edmund Welch, was published by Association Press.

1961. Annual meeting in Duluth, Minnesota. Professor Marshall L. Walters appointed Editor of *Guide* (handled preparation of material annually, 1962-1969 inclusive). Volleyball announced for the 1964 Olympic Games program in Tokyo. International Volleyball Federation (FIVB) adopted the USA plan of codifying the rules of the game.

1962. Philadelphia the scene of the annual meeting. Representatives from Division of Men's Athletics of AAHPER accepted on Board of USVBA. Criteria developed for selecting persons for regional "Honorable Mention" and listing in the *Guide.* IOC announced that a volleyball division for women, as well as men, would be on the Tokyo Olympic Games program. World championships conducted in Moscow: fifth time for men: won by USSR, second—Czechoslovakia; fourth time for women; won by Japan, second—USSR. *Beginning Volleyball,* by William T. Odeneal and Harry E. Wilson published by Wadsworth Publishing Company.

1963. Host for the annual meeting and championships was San Antonio, Texas. National Association of Intercollegiate Athletics (NAIA) accepted into USVBA membership. Pan American Games held in São Paulo, Brazil with volleyball included for third time; USA took second and Brazil was the winner in each division.

1964. Annual meeting, national championships, and Olympic squad selections held in New York City as part of the 1964-65 World's Fair. Church of Jesus Christ of Latter Day Saints (Mormon) accepted into USVBA membership. The USVBA participated, along with 29 other national sports bodies, in the USOC sponsored, Arthur D. Little, sports organization study. Olympic Games in Tokyo with volleyball included for first time: men's winner—USSR, second—Czechoslovakia, (USA—ninth); women's winner—Japan, second—USSR, (USA—fifth).

1965. Annual meeting held in Omaha, Nebraska, with championships conducted at Offutt Air Force Base (Strategic Air Command). Examined implications of USOC sponsored Arthur D. Little management study of sports for volleyball organization, leadership, financing, and long range development. Discussed a five-year plan proposed by Harry E. Wilson for improvement of volleyball coaches, players, and officials. USVBA "Frier Award" established by the Executive Committee and first presentation made during the Omaha meeting to Dr. Harold T. Friermood. Cross Canada matches played late in the fall between men's and women's teams from USA and USSR. Professor James E. Coleman, with State Department sponsorship, spent a month in Poland making an intensive study of volleyball training and coaching methods. USVBA met in New York City with representatives of fifteen USOC related sports organizations, to give broader interpretation of volleyball. Book, *Volleyball for Girls and Women,* by Betty Jane Trotter, published by Ronald Press.

1966. Annual meeting held in Grand Rapids, Michigan, with championships played at Calvin College. Plans made for volleyball in Pan American and Olympic Games, and beyond; programming and financing plans projected. A sound-color volleyball film made by local TV station. National Catholic Youth Organization Federation accepted into USVBA membership. Olympic Development meeting held in Washington, D.C., at NEA headquarters. Volleyball's long range plans presented and approved by USOC Committee on Development and the Board—allocation of $19,500 made for 1966-1968 period, $9,500 each to USOC men's and women's volleyball committees and $500 for "Volleyball Skills Program." The sixth world championships for men held in Prague in September: winner—Czechoslovakia, second—Romania (USA—eleventh). USA coaches made further study of European methods. "Volleyball Skills Program—for Olympic Development" booklet prepared; distributed through the regions and reproduced in annual *Guide.* USVBA sponsored a fiftieth anniversary limited edition issue of *When Volleyball Began—An Olympic Sport;* this carried a complete reproduction of the 1916 Spalding *Volleyball Guide,* selected highlights from the history of volleyball, the 1897 original rules first carried in the Handbook of the Athletic League of the YMCAs of North America, and an introductory statement by the anniversary edition editor.

1967. Fifth World Championships for Women held in Tokyo in January; results: first—Japan, second—USA. Japan's women's team visited USA in May for matches. Annual meeting held in Detroit, Michigan, with championships conducted in new gymnasiums of Wayne State University. Name of National Recreation Association changed during a major reorganization to National Recreation and Parks Association. Men's and Women's Pan American squads selected in Detroit; training program carried on in Minneapolis in July. Pan American Games held in Winnipeg, Manitoba, Canada; men's results: first—USA, second—Brazil, third—Cuba; Women's results: first—USA, second—Peru, third—Cuba. USVBA sponsored volleyball symposium was conducted in Los Angeles during Thanksgiving holidays to assemble "best current thinking" on volleyball coaching, playing, and officiating for wide distribution through the USVBA regions; E. B. DeGroot served as the organizer-director; project financed in part by USOC development funds.

1968. Fortieth USVBA anniversary meeting held in Portland, Oregon. Championships held in Portland State College's new gymnasium. The second USVBA "Frier Award" was presented to Harry E. Wilson. The USVBA was honored through presentations made by the National YMCA Health and Physical Education Committee, of historic medals from the 1919 Inter-Allied Games held in Paris, to past president Viggo O. Nelson, and current president, E. Douglas Boyden. Richard I. Caplan was recognized by the

USVBA for his participation as a player in thirty national championships. Emil W. Breitkreutz received commendation for his long service as chairman of the USVBA Committee on Equipment and Supplies. Eighteen players and alternates plus coaches and managers were selected and recommended for each of the men's and women's Olympic Games volleyball squads. Plans were approved for squad assembly and processing late in August in the Los Angeles locality with altitude training at South Lake Tahoe during September. Flying from Reno to Denver, then on to Mexico City, the twelve players for each team, with coaches and managers and internationally certified officials, participated in the Olympic Games. Men's results: first—USSR; second—Japan; USA took seventh. Women's results: first—USSR; second—Japan; USA took eighth.

During the early summer of 1968, a volleyball camp was conducted for the first time in the USA by the Columbus, Ohio YMCA at its Camp Willson near Bellefontaine, Ohio. This brought together about seventy-five players and coaches from ten states and three Canadian provinces. This was another landmark in the history of volleyball.

Throughout the forty-year history of the USVBA there has never been a paid executive. The work has always been carried on by enthusiastic volunteers, locally, throughout the regions, and nationally. An attempt to identify all these dedicated persons would not be possible. The following national positions are indicative of the interest and continuing contributions of thousands of volleyball workers and boosters.

Presidents of the USVBA

Dr. George J. Fisher (deceased), New York City, 1928-1952.
Dr. Harold T. Friermood, Pelham, New York, 1952-1955.
Viggo O. Nelson, Ann Arbor, Michigan, 1955-1959.
E. Douglas Boyden, San Antonio, Texas, 1959-.

Secretary-Treasurers of the USVBA

Dr. John Brown, Jr. (deceased), Miami, Florida, 1929-1943.
Dr. Harold T. Friermood, Pelham, New York, 1943-1951.
Merton H. Kennedy, Chicago, Illinois, 1951-1952.
Robert Morrison, Detroit, Michigan, 1952-1956.
Alton W. Fish, Long Beach, California, 1956-1962.
Wilbur H. Peck, New York City, 1962-1964.

Secretary of the USVBA

Wilbur H. Peck, New York City, 1964-.

Treasurers of the USVBA

Edward A. Heisler, Bethlehem, Pennsylvania, 1964-1967.
Leonard C. Gibson, Stockton, California, 1967-.

Editors of the USVBA ANNUAL REFERENCE GUIDE AND OFFICIAL VOLLEYBALL RULES

Dr. George J. Fisher (deceased), New York City, 1928-1949, with (Associate Editor) Robert E. Laveaga (deceased), Boston, Massachusetts, 1949.

Professor Marshall L. Walters, Springfield, Massachusetts, 1950-1953.

Logan C. Mundt, New York City, 1954-1958.

Dr. J. Edmund Welch, Atlanta, Georgia, 1959-1961.

Professor Marshall L. Walters, Boone, North Carolina, 1962-, with (Associate Editor) Professor Donald S. Shondell, Muncie, Indiana, 1969.

This quick survey suggests the stimulation and help given by the USVBA to many groups and the increasing national and international significance of the game. But in no sense does it reflect the developments that took place in each of the USVBA member organizations, nor record the personal enjoyment of the game resulting from skill improvement, recreative release from daily tensions, fitness and health developed, friendships made, and opportunity for service of many types. These things are deeply implanted in the lives of the participants.

Volleyball is a game that belongs to the people. This fierce sense of proprietorship is present be he player, teacher, coach, manager, official, spectator, reporter, man, woman, boy, or girl. Each says, "This is my game."

And so say I!

REFERENCES

1. Friermood, Harold T. "Sixty Years of Volleyball." Souvenir program—U.S. National Volleyball Championships, sponsored by YMCA, Oklahoma City, Oklahoma, 1955.
2. (First) "Rules of Volleyball." *Association Athletic League Handbook*, 1897. (Official Handbook of the Athletic League of the Young Men's Christian Associations of North America.)
3. Morgan, William G. "How Volley Ball Was Originated." *Official* (Guide) *Volley Ball Rules*. (Adopted by the Young Men's Christian Association Athletic League and the National Collegiate Athletic Association. Guide edited by Dr. George J. Fisher.) Spalding Athletic Library, Group XII, No. 364, American Sports Publishing Co., New York, N.Y., 1916.
4. (The Original) "Game of Volley Ball." *Physical Education*, July, 1896, pp. 50-51. (Reproduced in the 1916 Volleyball Rule Book, page 13.)
5. Selected annual volleyball guides: 1916 to 1968.

"The Spirit of Volleyball"

By HOWARD G. DANFORD and J. EDMUND WELCH*

VOLLEYBALL, in reality, has no spirit. It is only a game, and, as such, has potentialities for either good or evil, depending in a large degree upon the quality of the leadership involved. However, there is a distinctive spirit that characterizes the majority of the men and women who play volleyball.

The spirit of fun and good fellowship

First of all, the men and women who play this great game have fun playing it. The desire to win is not permitted to assume a position of such vast importance in the minds of the players that fun is replaced by grimness, relaxation by tension, and cordial friendships by bitter enmities. The players on opposing teams fraternize both before and after their matches. This type of cordial relationship is conspicuously absent in much of our intercollegiate and interscholastic athletics, particularly football. How many players on opposing college football teams ever meet each other except on the "field of battle"? We talk glibly of the social values in college sports, but for two football teams to sit down and eat their postgame meal together would necessitate a major revolution in the cerebral processes of present-day leaders in college football. Yet this spirit of good fellowship is the rule rather than the exception in volleyball.

The 1965 National Volleyball Championships were a typical example of the spirit of fun and fellowship which exists in this sport. There were one hundred and sixty-three matches, and not one formal protest was entered. In his analysis of the 1965 tournament, W. H. Peck concluded, "The friendliness and comradeship which is apparent between the players, coaches,

---

* The late Dr. Danford made very important contributions to volleyball while serving as athletic director at Florida State University, and he was the original author of this commentary. Dr. Welch made slight revisions and additions for the second edition of *How to Play and Teach Volleyball*.

and officials make this a championship unparalleled in the spirit of fellowship as well as keen competition."[1]

The spirit of amateurism

Volleyball is one of the few remaining amateur sports in America. There are no dollar signs suspended from the necks of volleyball players. They play for the sheer fun of playing—and this is the spirit of amateurism. Officials donate their services in many tournaments. This, too, is the spirit of amateurism elevated almost to a fantastic height.

The spirit of sportsmanship

The practice of spectators' booing officials or players is the rule in many sports, but is the exception at a volleyball tournament. Seldom have we seen examples of bad conduct on the part of players in a tournament, and, on those occasions, the players encountered strong disapproval from all the others present. Volleyball is played in a manner befitting ladies and gentlemen. There is no muckerism in volleyball, but unfortunately the same cannot be said of many other sports.

In describing the volleyball matches at the 1964 Olympic Games, Glen Davies wrote, *"Sportsmanship* was at its highest."[2]

The spirit of moral conduct

This, we believe, is perhaps the outstanding characteristic of volleyball today. When a player's finger barely touches the net, no official can possibly detect the foul. The player is faced with the necessity of making a moral choice between two diametrically opposed courses of action. Shall he conceal the foul or shall he admit it? This is a stern test of moral fiber, for admission of the foul may lose a national championship. But so high is the level of human conduct in this sport that the hand goes up immediately, even though there is no rule requiring him to do so.

> "One of the traditions of the game, developing as it did in the Holyoke, Massachusetts, YMCA in 1895, is that of personal responsibility and integrity in calling fouls—even when the referee, umpire, or linesmen fail to see violations. From this standpoint it is truly a player's sport and incidents in the topflight national competitions are on record where players have called their own fouls, missed by the officials, at times when it meant the difference between winning or losing the game and the match."[3]

In the finals of the 1960 National Volleyball Championships, Edward Williams called a foul on himself during a critical play. His team, the Hollywood YMCA Stars, eventually lost the match and national title to its arch rival, the Westside JCC of Los Angeles. After the match Williams was asked if he regretted admitting the foul. He replied, "My only regret is that I touched the ball. This is an honor sport, the officials can't see everything, so I had to call it."[4]

THE SPIRIT OF VOLLEYBALL

Harold T. Friermood, a long-time leader in the ethical facets of sports, expressed this moral conduct in volleyball as follows.

> "When such conduct is observed at a critical period in a contest, and fully understood, it stands out in the memory of players, spectators, and officials as the bright golden moment of that tournament. . . . It is a challenge greater than points, more important than winning a championship. It is love of the game, consideration for others, and mastery of fear of defeat."[5]

This type of conduct is Obedience to the Unenforceable, obedience to a moral code, a code of honor, a code of gentlemen. It is a kind of behavior so desperately needed in America today, for the true greatness of a nation is measured in large degree by the length and breadth of this area of human conduct in which men obey the unenforceable.

All this is "the spirit of volleyball," a spirit of which we who have had some small part in its development may well be proud.

REFERENCES

1. Peck, W. H., "U.S. Volleyball Championships—1965 Edition," *Journal of Physical Education*, July-August, 1965, p. 142.
2. Davies, Glen, "Impressions of Olympic Volleyball," *Journal of Physical Education*, January-February, 1965, p. 78.
3. Friermood, Harold T., "Volleyball Goes Modern," *Journal of Health, Physical Education, and Recreation*, May, 1953, p. 10.
4. Barta, Joe, "Fairest Foul Of Them All," *Journal of Physical Education*, September-October, 1960, p. 17 (published first in the May 15, 1960, issue of the *Dallas News*).
5. Friermood, Harold T., "Tribute to A. Provost Idell," *International Volleyball Review*, November-December, 1966, p. 8.

See also the following references:

A. Burton, Roger, "Honor and the Silent Sound," *International Volleyball Review*, June-August, 1967, p. 74.
B. Miller, C. L. Bobb, "Who Needs the Honor Call?" *Journal of Physical Education*, May-June, 1968, p. 139.
C. Shondell, Don, "Honor Call—Asset or Liability?" *International Volleyball Review*, June-August, 1967, p. 72.

DIAGRAM OF VOLLEYBALL COURT

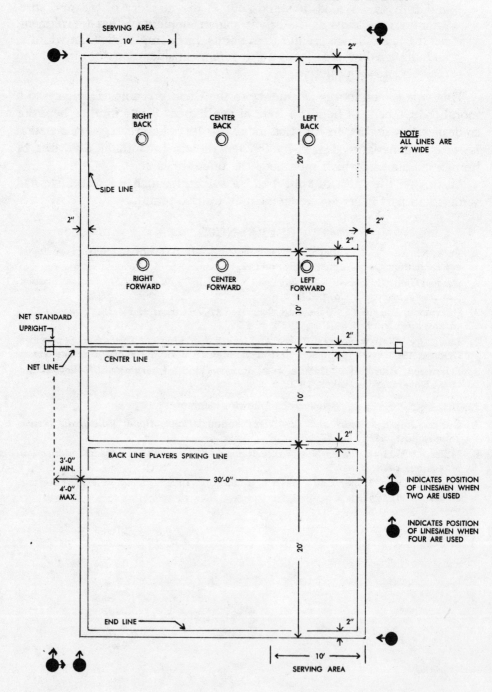

Used by permission from the 1968 *Official Volleyball Guide,* edited by Marshall L. Walters (Berne, Indiana: USVBA Printer).

1. Techniques of Serving the Ball

By JAMES C. DeWEESE, Jr.

WHEN the statement, "there is power in beginning," is applied to volleyball, it points up the importance of an effective serve. The beginning of a volleyball game is the serve. It is only when serving that a team can score points.

In order to play a powerful game of volleyball, individual players must develop an effective serve. They must have a serve that is a power both as an offensive weapon and defensive weapon. Whereas we shall differentiate on the offensive and defensive character of the serve later on in this chapter, the power referred to here is not only the force with which we strike the ball but the deceptive flight which the ball should take as it enters the opponents' court. Add to this deception accuracy of placement, and all of this goes into making a powerful serve.

The serve is the act of putting the ball in play by a player from the service area. (See service area as shown in Diagram of Volleyball Court.) This definition of the serve, which once appeared in the USVBA Rules, describes one of the most important plays in the game of volleyball. When this statement was first used in our rules, it very aptly described the serve, the attitude toward the serve, and, moreover, the effectiveness of the serve. Today, however, in our powerful, deceptive, and exciting game of volleyball, this definition falls far short of describing the serve. As the skills of the game have improved, certainly the complexity of the serve has increased to play its major role in the shaping of our present-day game. Odeneal, Wilson, and Wardale all stress the importance of the serve as a scoring weapon.[1] A simple statement in the *Canadian Volleyball Annual and Rule Book* sums up this viewpoint, "Control the serve and you control the game."[2]

There are many variations and types of serve. All of the variations can be grouped into three general types of serves—the underhand serve, the overhand serve, and the roundhouse serve. The effective use of these three types of serves has had a decided influence on the offensive strategy as well as the defensive strategy of the game. Because of this strong influence, the serve has also caused several changes to be made in the rules and will undoubtedly cause others.

UNDERHAND SERVE

In executing the underhand service, the server should be back of the end line and within the service area as defined in the rules. The server should stand with his knees flexed, and, in the case of a right-handed player, his left foot should be slightly in front of the right. The ball is held in the left hand to the front and right side of the body so that it will be directly in line with the right hand. A high back swing should be made with the right arm, and the forward swing should be made directly under the shoulder and through the ball. The elbow should be kept straight. The ball must be tossed slightly by the left hand, for the rules do not allow the server to hit the ball as a golf ball is hit off a tee. A good follow-through is essential. The right hand should be held like a claw, and the ball should be hit with the heel of the hand. Some players use a closed fist and hit the ball with the heel and flat surface of the fist, but it is difficult to have the control with the fist that one has with the open hand. As the swing is executed, a short step forward should be made with the left foot, shifting the body weight to the left foot. Special care should be taken to keep the foot from touching the end line, which would constitute a foot fault and result in the loss of serve. The foot fault admonition pertains to all types of serves, for "there is nothing more galling than to have a good serve disallowed through foot faulting."[3]

By continued practice, it is possible to hit the ball directly in the center, thus causing the ball to make its flight without any spinning or turning. This causes the ball to jump and slide, making a very effective serve. Even so, the underhand serve is not nearly as effective as an overhand serve.

It should be pointed out that the underhand serve is used mostly in the secondary school level and with individuals who do not have the strength and coordination necessary to execute the overhand serve. The better teachers and coaches start a player out with the overhand serve, and they resort to teaching the underhand serve only when it is evident that the individual player lacks the strength or coordination necessary for the overhand serve. In the Far Western Championships and the National Championships of 1965, only seven of 1,043 serves were underhand.[4]

OVERHAND SERVE

The overhand serve is a very effective serve and, with practice, can be very accurate. In preparing to serve, the server holds the ball in his left hand out in front of the right shoulder. The right hand is on the back side

Service by Dennis Johnson, a 1968 all-conference player for Ball State.

Photo: Donald S. Shondell and Ball State University.

of the ball, and the right arm should be in a position so that the upper arm is toward the frontal plane of the body and parallel to the floor. The serve is accomplished by tossing the ball easily to a position just above the level of the head and in front of the right arm and shoulder. The right hand should then be drawn back close to the head and behind the ear, and the hand should be held in a clawlike manner. The ball is hit in much the

37

Japanese woman player executes the roundhouse serve. It is not uncommon for some foreign players to stand 10 to 25 feet behind the end line when serving.

same manner as a spiker would hit a volleyball or in the same manner as a catcher might throw a ball to second base. The English author, Don Anthony, compares the overhand volleyball serve to the tennis serve.[5] The ball is hit with the heel of the hand and capped slightly with the fingers. There is very little follow-through on this service. Capping the ball with the fingers, after hitting it with the heel of the hand, will give a top spin to the ball, causing it to go at a fast rate similar to a spike. The ball may also be hit in the center and not capped with the fingers. This creates a floating ball that jumps and slides because it has no spin. Both the capped and the floater serves are very effective and can be used interchangeably.

Many fine servers toss the ball so that the valve is facing the front and is in the lower panel. The ball's flight is a dead float to about the net, but as the weight of the valve starts a spin in one direction or another the flight will become the wavering, swerving and unpredictable movement which is so effective.[6]

The most common stance of the server is with his feet in close proximity to and equidistant from the end line. However, some servers prefer to stand several feet behind the end line with one foot forward. It is not necessary to take a step with the overhand service. Here again, this is a matter of preference with the individual player.

The American players favor this overhand type of serve. At the 1968 National Championships, the hard overhand floater serve, with the server standing four to ten feet behind the end line, was the most common.[7]

Some of the better players are now employing a running approach toward the end line and hitting the ball as they run. This gives some extra speed to the ball, and it is somewhat more deceptive, but it also requires a much higher degree of skill and coordination. Players from Russia, Japan, Brazil, Peru, and Cuba use this serve, which is a variation of the overhand floater or a variation of the roundhouse serve.

ROUNDHOUSE SERVE

The roundhouse service can be one of tremendous power, or it can be one of medium speed. The mediocre players cannot utilize this serve without making too many costly errors. As noted above, foreign players use a variation of this serve and are successful with it.

In this service, the player should face the side line and be perpendicular to the end line. The ball is tossed straight up with both hands so that it will be directly over the right shoulder. The right arm is brought up from against the side, straight out and over the head, with the elbow kept straight. Contact is made with the ball at a point directly over the shoulder and with the heel of the open hand. The ball is capped with the fingers as it is hit. This causes the ball to go with only a slight rise, and with tremendous top spin, making it drop quickly as it crosses the net. The difficulty in returning the ball comes from its great velocity.

In the 1967 Pan American Games, the foreign players stood anywhere from a few feet back of the end line to 25 feet back. The deep position seemed to give them a better chance of keeping the ball in, but it should be stated that all servers were quite accurate. There were few net serves or "outs." The roundhouse or hook serve, which these players employed, traveled harder than the so-called American floater. It was interesting to note that the foreign players could also put a floating action to this roundhouse serve.

39

Fig. 1. Effective placement of hard, overhand floater serve in 1968 National Championships.

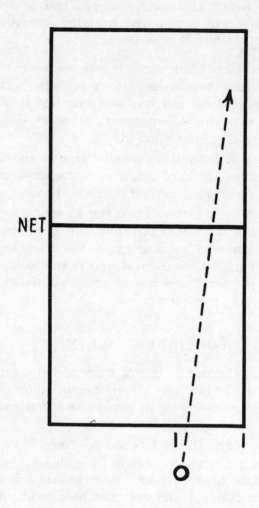

O — Player;   - - → Path of ball.

COMPARATIVE VALUE OF THE THREE SERVES

For many years the underhand serve was the basic or fundamental service in volleyball. Now this serve has been replaced in popularity by the overhand serve. Women players can and do learn the overhand serve, while practically all of the better men players use it.

Fig. 2. Roundhouse floater and hook serves are hit by such teams as Japan, Russia, and Brazil. Server stands 10 to 25 feet back from end line.

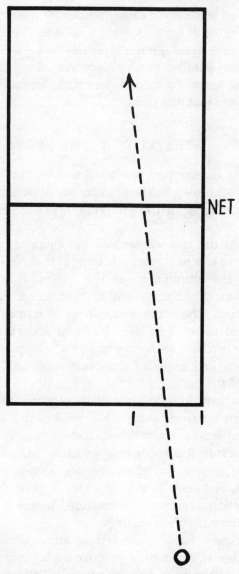

O — Player;   - - -→ Path of ball.

The underhand serve is of value at the secondary school level, but its value on the college level and above is questionable. The ball must travel in a relatively high arc to get over the net, and this gives the receiver time to move back for a deep serve or forward for a serve dropping over the net. The overhand serve is preferred because the good player can cause the ball to dip and slide, he can hit it in a flat trajectory, and he can be quite accurate with his placements.

American players have made little use of the roundhouse serve because they fear its inaccuracy and because the ball tends to travel in a straight line and hence can be received rather readily by the expert player. Although the roundhouse or hook serve is seldom used in this country, the fact that it is a common serve among foreign players indicates its importance to the game. During the coming years, more American players will probably adopt this type of serve. Foreign players have demonstrated that this serve can be accurate and can win points.

STRATEGY OF THE SERVE

The strategy of the serve in volleyball is ever changing. For many years the technique of screening the serve from the opposing team was employed in many ingenious ways. In 1965 the rule was changed, and the screen was made illegal.

This change in the rule eliminated the element of surprise that some teams were able to use to a great advantage. If there is any other effect on the game from the elimination of the screen, it is a positive force to improve the power of the serve and further refine other areas of strategy involving the serve. The three main areas of strategy with the serve are generally believed to be: (1) the consistent accuracy of serving the ball into the opponents' court without a foul, (2) the placement of the ball to individual players and areas of the court, and (3) the variation in the speed and path of the ball.

In order for a team to score, one of its players must first serve the ball successfully to the opposing team. This requires that the player must serve from the specified service zone without foot-faulting and that he hit the ball over the net and into the opponents' court. It would seem to be a rather simple matter to serve a volleyball over an eight-foot high net and into a 30' x 30' square, but such is not the case. A great deal of practice is required, and this first skill must be mastered before a player and his team can move on to more involved strategy.

Many players move back to the service area and serve with no thought of placement. This is a common practice even among some of the better players, and it contributes to fouls in serving. Taking a moment to aim the serve at a certain player, between players, or to a certain area of the court will pay dividends in accurate serving. Attempts at placement increase the accuracy of the serve. At the 1968 National Championships, Shondell noted that "the good servers took time to concentrate on each serve, and accuracy of placement was amazing."[8]

If a team has a poor ball handler, it is good strategy to hit the serve to this player. As long as he commits fouls, the serves should be directed to him. This hurts his confidence and the morale of his teammates. If his teammates try to cover for him, this usually contributes to poor teamwork or creates an open space.

The better teams have players who are all good ball handlers. In playing against such teams, the best strategy is to hit the serve between two players and cause them to move to the ball. This may lead to indecision or mistakes on their part as to which player will take the ball. Indecision on the part of two players may cause the ball to fall between them to the floor. A mistake in judgment may result in the two players colliding and playing the ball poorly.

The short serve just clearing the net is a good serve, providing the server can be consistently accurate and not serve into the net. The value of this short serve, however, is further reduced because the majority of the serves today are received with the double forearm or bump pass. If the ball is served short, this requires the receiver to make only a short pass to his setter, which in turn enables the opposing team to muster a quick attack.

It is generally felt among the leading teachers and coaches that the deep serve is by far the best strategy. This requires the receiver to move backward, and this, in most cases, is an awkward position. Moving away from the ball increases the probability of having the ball come to rest in the receiver's hands, which is a foul. If a bump-type play is attempted, this requires making the play above the head. The bump pass is best executed with the ball in front of the player and at a height well below the waist.

The difficulty of playing the ball can be increased further by requiring the player to move to his right or left as he goes backward. The skill of placing the ball in all of these different areas is the mark of a good server. The good server's effectiveness is also seen as he continues to change the placement of his service. This small change will, to some degree, make the returning of a serve difficult.

The difficulty of receiving the service can be compounded by varying the speed and flight of the serve. A fast serve is difficult to handle because of its velocity and because it may be somewhat unexpected. This being true, a slow or soft serve can, from time to time, be effective, also.

The floating serve that dips and slides is generally believed to be the best of the serves. It tends to fool the receiver just as a knuckle ball pitch in baseball fools the batter. The fact that this serve can be served as a soft serve or as a power serve is another reason why it is used so widely and is so effective.

The employment of these few aspects of strategy in the serve make it a part of the game that must be considered as more than simply the beginning of a point. The offensive nature of the serve is well known, for good servers win many points in volleyball with the serve alone.

The serve is also a potent defensive weapon. The player who serves the ball effectively can cause his opponents to make a weak return or actually play the ball back to an area his team prefers. In this sense, the serve is defensive because it has rendered impotent the offense of the opponents.

Few players and teams master all of the principles and skills of serving, but those who do are more likely to attain top ratings in state, area, national, and international competition. Many are average and some are good, but all should strive constantly to be the best. Every part of volleyball is important to the game, so whatever you are doing—serving, passing, spiking—work at it, concentrate on it, and be the best.

REFERENCES

1. Odeneal, William T., and Wilson, Harry E., *Beginning Volleyball* (Belmont, California: Wadsworth Publishing Company, Inc., 1962), p. 16, and Wardale, Peter, *Volleyball: Skills and Tactics* (London: Faber and Faber Limited, 1964), p. 38.
2. Bratton, Robert D., ed., *1965 Canadian Volleyball Annual and Rule Book* (Scarborough, Ontario, Canada: CVA Publications), p. 33.
3. Wardale, *op. cit.*, p. 61.
4. Jensen, Clayne R., and Dotson, Larry, "An Analysis of Serving Methods in Volleyball," *Athletic Journal*, March, 1966, p. 34.
5. Anthony, Don, *Volleyball: Do It This Way* (London: John Murray Company, 1964), pp. 18-19.
6. Boyden, E. Douglas, Burton, Roger G., and Odeneal, William T., *Volleyball Syllabus* (Pacific Palisades, California: P. O. Box 514, c/o Betty Ghormley, 1961), p. 2.
7. Shondell, Donald S., personal correspondence, May 18, 1968.
8. *Ibid.*
   For an excellent description of serving techniques, see also the following reference:
   Odeneal, William T., "What Ails U.S. Volleyball?" *Amateur Athlete*, April, 1965, pp. 14, 28, 29.

2. Techniques of Passing the Ball

By MURRELL EDMUNDS and J. EDMUND WELCH

IN our treatment of passing techniques, we are concerned mainly with methods of receiving the serve, such as the overhand pass* and double forearm or bump pass. The set constitutes a separate phase of passing the ball and will be covered in Chapter 3. Other methods of keeping the ball in play by expert defensive measures, such as various bump and dig passes, are covered in the chapter on defense.

The so-called "pass" in volleyball constitutes the most controversial part of the game. This is true because the rules require that the ball must be clearly hit. It cannot be held, lifted, or scooped, and the official must make a split-second decision on the matter.

Before World War II, even the best players resorted to hitting a low ball with their palms turned upward. This technique is never used by the champion player of today, but, unfortunately, it is still employed often in instructional and recreational volleyball. The "gap" between championship volleyball and the volleyball of YMCA classes, intramural, church, and industrial leagues, and physical education classes in junior high, senior high, and college, is greatest in this single phase of the sport.

Even among leading volleyball authorities, there is much debate concerning what constitutes a legal pass, especially when a player receives the serve. As late as the 1964 United States National Championships, our top players used the traditional overhand pass when receiving the serve. In the 1964 Olympic Games, our coaches and players found foreign referees calling this action a foul. The best foreign teams, such as Russia and

---

* In past years the overhand pass has been described by a number of terms such as chest pass, face pass, and overhead pass. The 1967 National Volleyball Coaches Symposium has recommended the term, "overhand pass."

45

Japan, were "bumping" the first ball with the double forearm pass. Since the officials were ruling against the overhand pass on serve receptions and allowing the "bump pass," some leading American coaches and players abandoned the former technique and adopted the latter.

Both the International Volleyball Federation (FIVB) and the United States Volleyball Association (USVBA) have viewed this development with alarm. Each of these ruling bodies issued directives in 1966 stating that the overhand pass should be allowed in service receptions. Individual volleyball authorities have backed these directives. These include Vladimir Savvin, president of the U.S.S.R. Volleyball Federation and chief of officials at the 1967 Pan American Games; E. Douglas Boyden, president of the U. S. Volleyball Association and chairman of the U. S. Olympic Committee for Men's Volleyball; and Harry E. Wilson, coach of the 1964 U. S. Olympic Men's Team and coach of more U. S. national championship teams than any other person.

In the December, 1967, issue of the *Athletic Journal,* the editor of this book published a controversial article on the overhand pass entitled, "Volleyball Chest Pass Is Dead?" The veteran volleyball leader, Harry Wilson, who serves as a vice president of the International Volleyball Federation, reviewed a prepublication draft of the article and responded strongly as follows.

> I don't think the chest pass is dead; nor do I think it ever will be. I think it is a basic part of the game. . . . The members of the International Volleyball Federation are doing everything they can to discourage the calling of the chest pass as being illegal in receiving the serves or saving a hard-driven spike. . . .[1]

In view of these official directives, the opinions of the authorities mentioned here, and our personal belief that the overhand or chest pass is an integral part of the game, we take the position that the player should make a determined effort to utilize this technique in receiving the serve. We recognize that the bump pass is no longer primarily a recovery shot as it was when the first edition of *How to Play and Teach Volleyball* was published. Championship players are very skillful with the bump pass and can direct the first ball successfully to the setter. Our primary concern is the fact that officials have practically eliminated the overhand pass from championship play by faulty rule interpretations. If this were not so, then the FIVB and the USVBA would not have issued the directives of 1966.

Our secondary concern is for the instructional program in the secondary schools and in the colleges. The top teams may abandon the overhand pass completely, but this technique will be used by schools and colleges for many years to come. We believe we have an obligation to present to these thousands of players the proper method of executing the overhand pass, particularly as it pertains to serve receptions. With this historical overview, we now present our concepts concerning "Techniques of Passing the Ball."

THE PASS: ITS IMPORTANCE

A truism which cannot be too often repeated is this: *team success in any competitive sport demands a mastery of fundamentals*. This generality, important in so many games, is particularly relevant to volleyball, where basic procedures are repeated over and over again, endlessly, on both attack and defense, on both sides of the net, and in a numberless variety of situations.

The fundamentals of volleyball are usually listed as these: the serve, the block, and *the big three* (the game's *great triumvirate*) of the attack: the pass, the set, the spike. This discussion will be concerned essentially with *the pass*, which is the attempt to hit the ball to the setter who in turn sets it up for the spiker. It must be said at once that the nature of the game is such that none of the closely integrated techniques of *the big three* may be entirely divorced from the others, even in theory. The pass, the set, and the spike are parts of a whole, like separate members of the same body, and they are interwoven in such a closely knit pattern that when one fails to function properly, the others suffer, sometimes beyond repair.

The *bridge* between passer, setter, and spiker is skillful *ball handling*, magic words to be noted well and remembered long. "The importance of the fundamentals of ball handling should be introduced and taught immediately, since ball handling is the key to a successful game."[2]

The man who is responsible for keeping this bridge in good repair is the passer. Perhaps his most difficult passing assignment occurs when he receives the serve. The passer is not a man whose excellence is appreciated by the galleries, and in this respect he may be likened to the blocking back in football—a man who prepares the way for the climax of the *attack*. The finest running back is of little avail if his blockers fail to do their work and leave him unprotected from the assaults of defensive tacklers. Likewise, the proudest spiker in the Olympic Games can be frustrated if a hopelessly bad pass is slapped into the face of his setter, who is, therefore, unable to make a decent set.

Trotter has presented a very appropriate summary of the place of the pass.

> The Pass is the beginning of the attack, regardless of the offensive pattern of play developed by the team. No good offensive play can possibly result without a sound beginning in a good pass . . . any experienced player, teacher, coach, official, or spectator knows that the Pass—emphasizing the proper distance to the Key-Set; the necessary height to permit that player to get under the ball and be waiting for it, and the reduction of spin and force—is an absolute essential. It is also known that the player who has been able to master this skill has worked long and hard, for despite its apparent ease, it requires dedicated and diligent practice to perfect.[3]

Tony Musica demonstrates the overhand pass. Musica was 1968 Midwest Intercollegiate Volleyball Association's "Most Valuable Player."

Photo: Donald S. Shondell and Ball State University.

Some of the specialized techniques of ball handling will be treated later in this chapter, but we desire to comment briefly on the subject here.

The wise player will eliminate completely from his repertoire the two-handed contact of low balls with the palms of the hands turned upward, thumbs out, and backs of the hands flat toward the floor. Whereas the ball can be legally hit with this underhand pass, the practice is not recom-

48

mended for two reasons. First, the overhand pass, the bump pass, and the dig pass are much more efficient means of playing the ball. Wardale refers to the overhand pass as "the most accurate and the easiest pass to control,"[4] while bump and dig passes allow a player to cover a much greater range than does the "palms up" underhand pass. Second, this underhand

Westside JCC of Los Angeles in preparatory formation for receiving the serve. Players, left to right, are Ronnie Lang, Gene Selznick, Dick Hammer, and Larry Scott. Lang, especially, shows the poised but relaxed form which is recommended. Body is low, weight is slightly forward, arms and hands are relaxed and out in front, and eyes are on the approaching serve. Selznick is beginning his move to the front line to become the setter in 5-1 (three spiker) offense.

pass leads to many ball-handling fouls. The rules forbid the ball to visibly come to rest.

    . . . it is commonly known that a player is most likely to allow the ball to visibly come to rest if he plays the ball with the palms of two hands underhand, from behind his shoulder, from behind his head, or overhead with his back to the net. A ball played in this manner acts as a red light and should cause any official to look very closely for visible rest at contact. It is possible to play it lawfully, but it is poor playing technique to follow consistently.[5]

Jane Ward, captain of the U.S. Women's Team in Pan American Games and Olympic Games, moves to receive the serve with an overhand pass. Her fingers, hands, and arms are in the classic position. She is off balance, but fine utilization of the hands and wrists enables the champion to make such a play.

METHOD: THE OVERHAND PASS

The best method of handling the pass is the overhand technique. The arms are extended upward, palms of the hands outward toward the ball, thumbs pointed toward each other and nearly touching, fingers wide to form with palms and heels of the hands a concave basket, and elbows forward of the body to form with the forearms and upper arms a flexible oval. Some players prefer to keep the arms and elbows extended out in front of the body in line with the shoulders, especially when receiving the serve. Others prefer to have the arms and elbows in a more relaxed position near the chest.

The skillful passer learns to get his body in position to make this pass whenever possible, moving forward or backward or to the sides. His legs are apart, slightly flexed, with one foot forward. He will not hesitate to

Barbara Perry, U.S. Pan American and Olympic Games player, executes the forearm or bump pass. Players will not hesitate to hit the floor after making this pass. They do a "Jap" roll and come up quickly to their feet, ready to play.

51

squat down for low balls or even drop to one knee. In some cases when he must do a deep squat, he will give with the ball, fall backwards on his buttocks, execute a backward roll, and come up quickly, ready to play. Although Lowell stresses the deep squat in relation to diving saves, his reference is equally applicable when using the overhand pass on low balls, ". . . the *skill* of getting *low* is a vital part of the game. Therefore, any player who wishes to excel at the game must learn to 'dust the floor' with his trunks in the deep squat position. . . ."[6]

On more traditional serve receptions, the extended arms of the passer gradually retract and follow the approaching ball in until it reaches face level. Here the ball is struck with the fingers as the wrists give slightly, and in one continuous movement the ball is clearly batted with the fleshy parts of the fingers and thumbs. Wrist and finger action, not body action, is the most vital part of the overhand pass. Whereas many changes have occurred in volleyball during the past decade, Burton's analysis of the Hollywood YMCA Stars in 1959 is just as true today as it pertains to the correct technique of executing this pass, "The wrists cock backward just before the ball is hit and then the fingers roll forward as the ball is struck. Their warm-up drills stress this wrist snap roll."[7]

It is common to refer to a star football end as having "great hands." The expert volleyball passers, such as Ronnie Lang, Harlan Cohen, Gene Selznick, and Rolf Engen, have possessed "great hands." This talent has enabled them to make accurate passes even when off balance.

One final point needs to be made concerning technique. It is wise to avoid contacting the ball on the palms or on the heels of the hands, both out of consideration for accuracy in directing the ball, and in order to avoid a possible call by the referee for holding, pushing, or lifting. The overhand pass is the good player's bread-and-butter tool, and he should practice it incessantly.

METHOD: THE FOREARM PASS

The 1967 National Volleyball Coaches Symposium has defined the double forearm or bump pass as follows.
Forearm Pass. A ball played in an underhand manner. The forearms held away from the body will act as a surface from which the pass can be made.

Among championship teams, the double forearm pass is the most common technique at the present time in receiving the serve. It is also used to "dig" spikes, particularly those coming straight at the defensive player or fairly close to his right or left.

Carl M. McGown of The Church College of Hawaii, who studied volleyball in Poland, has provided this description of how to execute the double forearm pass:

The forearm pass is composed of two distinct phases: (1) hand, arm, and body position, and (2) passing technique.

Position. The back of one hand is placed in the other with the fingers of one hand perpendicular to the fingers of the other; the thumbs parallel and very close together. The elbows are *completely straight* and rotated in toward each other, forcing the flat surfaces of the forearms upward. The arms are held in front of and in the center of the body, extended slightly away from the body. The hands should be at or just above knee level. The feet are in a stride position approximately shoulder width apart, knees well bent.

Technique. The ball is contacted in the forearm area, not on the hands. The forearms are level and contact the ball simultaneously. The ball is hit with total body action, with the movement of the arms coming from the shoulders and not the elbows.[9]

In a match between the Cuban and Mexican women's teams during the 1967 Pan American Games, Coach Harlan Cohen observed that the positioning of the players was excellent as they prepared to receive serves by means of the double forearm pass.* When receiving, both sides were poised and alert. Their hands were down and their bodies were kept low.

In 1959 most, but not all, of the championship players were able to use the double forearm pass effectively. Now *all* players who aspire to compete at the national and international level must master the double forearm pass. If the overhand pass returns as the basic technique in receiving the serve, the importance of the double forearm pass will not be lessened. The double forearm pass is as much a part of modern volleyball as is the overhand floater serve or the power spike.

CONCLUSION

A spiker is a specialist whose basic skill can be used only under certain specific conditions, and so is the setter. But *every* member of a team is a *passer,* and there is no way he can avoid his responsibilities. *He* is the man who initiates the attack, and if he does a bad, slovenly job, then the whole pattern of offense is bogged down. It is not a glamorous role, but it is an essential one. It is almost axiomatic that a good pass leads to a skillful set which, in turn, results in a decisive spike. And, alas, conversely!

The role of the passer calls for a special kind of sportsmanship, an austere, self-discipline—one which places team success above personal applause, one where the reward comes not from the shouts of approval of unperceptive onlookers, but from the quiet satisfaction of a difficult skill mastered by constant practice and utilized for the group good.

---

* Harlan Cohen coached the USA Women's Team to first place honors in the 1967 Pan American Games.

REFERENCES

1. Wilson, Harry E., personal correspondence, September 12, 1967.
2. Tom, Marilynn C., and Luckman, Margaret N., *Coed Volleyball* (Palo Alto, California: The National Press, 1966), p. 3.
3. Trotter, Betty Jane, *Volleyball for Girls and Women* (New York: The Ronald Press Company, 1965), p. 21.
4. Wardale, Peter, *Volleyball: Skills and Tactics* (London: Faber and Faber Limited, 1964), p. 29.
5. Walters, Marshall L., ed., *1968 Official Volleyball Guide* (Berne, Indiana: USVBA Printer), pp. 155-156.
6. Lowell, John C., "Volleyball as a Combative Sport" (unpublished syllabus, 1967), The Church College of Hawaii, Laie, Hawaii, p. 19.
7. Burton, Roger G., "Coast Sweeps Play in Ioway," *International Volleyball Review*, May-June, 1959, p. 49.
8. McGown, Carl M., ed., *It's Power Volleyball* (Pacific Palisades, California: P. O. Box 514, c/o Betty Ghormley, 1968), p. 4.
9. *Ibid.*, p. 8.

See also the following references:

A. Leibrock, Philip, "Volleyball the Right Way," *Scholastic Coach,* December, 1965, p. 30.
B. Welch, J. Edmund, "Volleyball Chest Pass Is Dead?" *Athletic Journal,* December, 1967, pp. 24-25, 41, 42.

3. Techniques of Setting the Ball

By J. EDMUND WELCH

"Pass, *set, spike—pass, set, spike*" are the offensive fundamentals to be drilled into the novice volleyballer, improved in the mediocre player, and admired in the great player. Without the effective execution of all three maneuvers, no volleyball team can muster a winning offense. Without a good pass, the set is usually bad. Without a good set, the spike is usually bad. Without a good spike, both the pass and the set can become futile efforts. It is impossible to say that one is more important or less important than another in obtaining the point or the ball as the case may be. The spike appears more glamorous, the pass can appear more difficult in unusual recoveries, but the set undoubtedly requires more precise co-ordination of the muscles and reflexes. All are important and all must be practiced constantly to attain a balance of efficiency.

The importance of the set is illustrated in Peck's appraisal of play in the 1968 National Open Championships. "The key to modern offense is good setting. Consistently throughout the tournament, poor setting was deter-minate in the outcome of a match."[1] After James E. Coleman viewed the World's Cup Championships in 1965, he had this to say about setting:

> In my opinion, the world's championships are decided first on defense and second on setting . . . if I were asked to name the best players in the World's Cup, I would name four setters. The Russians had two great ones in Poyerkof and Vengierofski, the Poles had Sivek and the Japanese had Demachi. These men were not only magicians with the ball, but they were sensational diggers and very adequate blockers.[2]

In this chapter we are concerned with the volleyball set—its purpose, the player, the mechanics, and various other technical aspects of its use.

55

PURPOSE

The sole purpose of the set is to place the ball in position in relation to the net from which the most effective spike can be made. Whereas there is much difference of opinion as to what constitutes the best height, the best direction, the best distance from the net, the best arc of fall, and the best floor target for which the setter should aim his set, there can be little disagreement with the premise that the best set ball is the one which enables the spiker to make an effective spike. To enable the spiker to make an effective spike must be the intention of the set. The set is not the blow which obtains a point, and therefore must be considered a supporting play. A reasonable consistency in setting the ball in a position in relation to the net from which the most effective (not necessarily the hardest) spike can be made fulfills the purpose of the set. Strategy and application must not confuse this purpose. It should be pointed out that a team must vary the set intentionally when the blocking gets tough. "The setter today must be able to vary the attack by setting different types of balls. The 'Jap' set, the low set, and the 'shoot' set must be in his repertoire."[3]

QUALITIES DESIRED IN THE PLAYER

Just as in any other brand of endeavor, perfection in volleyball play or the perfect player is only an ideal, an impossible attainment. There are basic qualities which a coach seeks in a setter, however; these are only a few of a long list of desired qualities.

Competitive spirit is placed at the head of the list. In the beginning it is not necessary that such spirit and desire be for the attainment of excellence in volleyball. Such a spirit is usually already evident in the rawest recruit through his attainments in other sports, such as basketball, track, and tennis. Seldom does one find a player intensely interested in volleyball at the outset, but if the competitive spirit, the drive, the desire to excel, are there, then such a player will soon develop a specific competitive spirit for excellence in volleyball if given the proper urging. Regardless of a player's abilities in other sports, it is essential for a setter or volleyball player in general to develop this specific competitive spirit in volleyball, or he will not be very good at the game.

Mental alertness comes second. Where is the net? Where are the blockers? Which spiker should be used? Where will my set be? These and many other questions will flash through the setter's mind and must be answered instantly, even instinctively. Of course, there is a premium to be placed on consistency in a setter's actions, but such consistency must make allowances for constantly developing variations during the course of the play. Such variations are so frequent in the course of fast-moving play that a setter must be mentally alert if he is to avoid the errors of mental lapses, so damaging to a team's morale.

Instinctive reaction time is difficult to differentiate from mental alertness. Often there is no time to answer all the questions logically, nor is it even necessary to do so. It is the instinctive reaction, the quickness of muscle coordination that will put a setter in balance with a bad pass, under a spiked ball, or in blocking position. Experience is helpful in developing the psychology necessary for a good instinctive reaction time, but it is not the whole answer. Advancing years show up quickest in a volleyball player in this particular phase of his play.

Mobility, good anticipation, and *speed* rate high in the qualities of a setter, and work hand in hand with mental alertness and instinctive reaction time. He must reach his proper position, often changing direction en route, to execute his play faster than any other single player as a general rule. Short passes, low passes, and high passes to the setter and difficult spike recoveries by the setter are so frequent as to make the routine warm-up type of set position an academic ideal seldom seen after the game starts. Even when the pass to the setter is good, he must usually recover his proper position from a block or from being pulled into a spiking defense or serve defense position.

Coolness under fire usually comes with experience in competitive play. Although volleyball is unique in many ways and experience is a quality that cannot be lightly regarded, this particular trait of coolness under fire can be developed in other sports. The player with the tendency to blow up or pull mental blunders when the score gets close and the time is about up will lose the close ones for a team. This particular trait is not confined to setters but seems to be accentuated by the position. Tied-up muscles when attempting short, low sets and faulty sets over the net are common evidences of the lack of coolness under fire. Some players get better when the going gets rough and some get worse. Coolness under fire is the stabilizing factor in the man with the high emotional, competitive spirit, as contrasted with a smart player who lets the closeness of the play affect his logical thinking.

Endurance can be drilled into a player by proper training. Too few volleyballers are in condition to play the long, hard matches made necessary by the usual type of tournament. Many of the better volleyball teams are defeated in the latter stages of important tournaments simply because they become too tired to go the distance. This problem is not volleyball's alone, but it is so evident and so commonplace to the game because of the lack of proper training methods and the lack of intelligent use of team personnel. These remarks do not pertain to the great volleyball powers such as Russia, Poland, and Japan, and to the top five or six teams in the United States. The U.S. teams which won the men's and women's championships of the 1967 Pan American Games were in superb physical condition.

Size is placed last, not because of its importance but because of its lack of importance. There are many traits too innumerable to discuss here which in their way are important to the setter, but size in itself is not one of

Gene Selznick, twice named the Most Valuable Player in the National Open Championships, prepares to set for spiker. Ball is in perfect relationship to hands, head, and chest. Although Selznick is slightly off balance, he demonstrates cardinal principle employed by great setters —he controls the ball with fingers and wrists, not with his entire body. This enables the setter to set fair passes as well as good ones.

these traits. It makes no difference how large or how small a man is in physical stature in order to be a good setter. On the contrary, all too often the setter is chosen simply because he is "too short" to be a spiker. There is no person too tall to set and none too short to play volleyball.

If we think of the relative importance in point getting of the spiker and the setter, consider that the latter handles the ball twice as much on the front line as does the former, and with much more precision and accuracy in ball handling. Why then must we always allow a player equally good at spiking and setting to be a spiker when logic tells us he would be more valuable to the team as a setter?

All things being equal, one cannot deny that height is of great advantage for the setter when he must block. More and more of the leading teams are using tall men as setters. This was illustrated in the finals of the 1968 National Open Championships. The Westside JCC of Los Angeles, who defeated the Hawaii Outriggers for the title, "benched one of the best setters in the game to go with a starting lineup that averaged over 6'3"."[4]

MECHANICS OF THE SET

Position prior to set

Body balance is the most important directive in the proper set of a volleyball. While exact positions of various parts of the body are enumerated below, any other positions enabling coordinated muscular movement from a balanced body are acceptable and will produce good sets if the arc of the passed ball falls through the center of body balance from a position well above the setter's head.

The balls of the feet should equally support the body weight. Heels of both feet should be touching the floor, but supporting no weight. One foot should be about ten inches in front of the other. The feet should be about twelve inches apart, but that will be determined by the player in relation to body balance.

Legs are slightly bent and are flexible. The body should be straight without stiffness. The shoulders will be naturally drawn in slightly by the position of the arms but should not be humped forward.

Head and neck will be governed by the fall of the ball. Normally, contact with the ball will be made just before it would strike the nose. Arms from shoulder to elbow should be on a level with shoulders and slightly forward. Arms from elbow to wrist will be angled slightly upward so as to place the thumbs near and on a level with the nose.

Wrists should be flexible, yet bent back almost ninety per cent to allow palms of the hands to be upward from the floor. Fingers should be flexible and extended but not joined. All of the weight of the ball should be taken on fleshy parts of the fingers, most of the weight being concentrated on the thumbs and index fingers, while the remaining fingers act as directional guides. In setting, the ball should never touch the palms of the hands.

Contact with ball and follow-through

Contact with the ball and follow-through is a coordinated muscle movement of wrists and fingers, arms, shoulders, knees and legs, and balls of feet, all designated to clearly bat the ball with a smooth, light touch to the desired height and position in relation to the net. Careful consideration and practice should be devoted to eliminate: (1) jerky muscles causing height and direction errors, (2) lifting the ball—usually caused by allowing ball to strike palms of hands or by late arm reflex, and (3) a spinning ball—caused by too much wrist and finger action.

Ronnie Lang executes the back set to the spiker, Mike Bright. Both players have been All-Americans and have represented the U.S. in the Olympic Games.

Just as in passing, some great setters employ a technique emphasizing arms, wrists, and fingers. Very little body action is noticeable. E. B. DeGroot, Jr., who was manager of the U.S. Men's Team in the 1964 Olmpic Games, emphasized this point when he wrote, "The more big muscles that get into the act, the more inaccurate it may be."[5]

Back set

There is a marked similarity in body position prior to the routine front set and the over-the-head or back set. In the first place, there is no necessity for a different stance, and, in the second place, a different stance would tip off the direction of the set and destroy the surprise element.

Differences occur upon contact with the ball and are as follows. The arc of the pass should be judged so as to be set off the forehead instead of the nose, the neck should be bent more sharply up and back to follow properly the flight of the ball, and the wrists should be bent back more than in the front set so that the fingers handle the set direction more than the thumbs. With his fingers laid back, the setter can direct the ball behind him by means of an upward and backward movement of the hands.

Egstrom and Shaafsma recommend a sound technique to add deception as to whether or not the set will go forward or backward. From the normal stance, the setter can take a step back as the ball is contacted and set to the spiker in front of him. If he takes a step forward, he can easily set to the spiker behind him. The setter should delay taking this step until the last second in order to keep the opposing blockers unaware of which spiker will be receiving the ball.[6]

Other sets

The normal overhand set, either forward or backward, is not the only legal set. Any clearly batted ball is permissible. Some of these are as follows.

A. *Double forearm or bump set.* The technique of the double forearm set is similar to that of the double forearm pass described in Chapter Two. For situations when the overhand set is impossible because the pass is too low or too wide, the double forearm set provides the most practical alternative.

B. *Moving set.* By moving set, we mean that the setter is not planted in the normal position when he executes the set. Offenses which require the setter to move from the back line to the front line often find him setting "on the move." These setting situations require expert hand and wrist action.

C. *"Jap" set.* This set gets its name from the Japanese who use it with effectiveness. The spiker has already begun his jump as the setter feeds him a quick, low set. This enables the spiker to smash the ball before the blockers get up in the air. There is nothing new to the "Jap" or "pop" set. It was used as early as 1950 by the Mexicans. Fine timing on the part of both the setter and spiker is necessary for this play to work.

D. *Low set.* Whereas a normal set goes from five to eight feet above the net, a low set goes about three feet. Once again, it is designed to "beat the blockers to the draw," but it does not require the precise timing of the "Jap" set.

E. *Shoot set.* This is a low, fast set usually from the right forward position all the way across to the left forward position. This, too, can fool the blockers who may be expecting the setter to set to the middle forward.

F. *Back-line set.* Sometimes because of a deflection of the first pass, a back-line player is called upon to set. This requires a long set to a spiker at the front line, and it is a difficult maneuver. The ball must be set in front of the spiker.

G. *Jump set.* An example of the jump set occurs when a team is able to set the first pass to a spiker. The spiker jumps in the air to smash the ball, sees opposing blockers forming in front of him, and quickly changes his tactics in midair by setting the ball across to another spiker.

TECHNICAL ASPECTS AND STRATEGY

Perfect qualities of the player and thorough application of the mechanics are the goals of good setters. It takes more, however, to be a great setter.

He is the brains of the offense. He chooses the direction of the spike and the spiker's most effective play in any given position. He is in the best position to know if a spiker is getting a reasonable set. He knows if the passes are short or too low, indicating weakness in the back line. Accordingly, he knows best the capabilities of his teammates, their temperaments, and physical condition. He is able to observe the weaknesses and strong points of the opposing defense. Proper use of this knowledge will enable him to make more effective use of his spikers. If he can add to this a flair for doing what is unexpected to the opposition but in coordination with the capabilities of his teammates, the resulting surprise action will win many plays.

Where should the set be in relation to the side line? *Normally,* the arc of the ball should be such that the spiker makes contact with the ball about 36 inches inside the court, whether it be the right or left side.

How high should the ball be set? *Normally,* the ball should be set between five and eight feet above the net, the height being in direct relationship to the distance of the setter from the spiker. When players are first learning how to spike, setters should strive to set the ball at a consistent height. This makes the ball easier to hit. As mentioned previously, the height of sets should be varied in good competition. Sets of consistent height give the opposing blockers the advantage of knowing when the spike will be hit. This makes the job of blocking easier.

Good spikers who practice can hit sets of two or three different heights. First they learn by a system of signals with the setter. Later they develop a sense of intuition as to when sets of varying heights are coming. Signals can be important, though, even in top-flight competition. At the 1968 National Open Championships, Shondell reported, "The spikers on the top teams were always ready to hit and often worked with predetermined signals, either visual or audible, to communicate with the setter as to where and what kind of set."[7]

How far from the net should the set be? *Normally*, the ball should be set from two to four feet back from the net. Now that blockers may reach over the net, sets closer than two feet are especially vulnerable to being blocked. If the opposition blocking is highly ineffective, the ball can be set near the net. Once again, there are exceptions to the matter of sets close to the net. The "Jap" set is placed close to the net; and Larry Rundle, Most Valuable Player of the 1968 National Open Championships, hit close sets with such a sharp inside cut that his spikes often barely missed the blockers.[8]

Should a setter directly play the ball which has been hit over the net by the opposition? *Normally*, the setter should avoid making this play if another player can make a reasonable pass. *Occasionally*, a setter may choose to eliminate the pass from the fundamental pass-set-spike by setting the first ball. This is a difficult but very effective play when properly executed.

When should the setter not take the first pass from a teammate? He should not set the ball when it is passed away from his normal position. In this instance the player closest to the ball should set it, and the usual setter should get ready to spike.

When should a setter spike the first or third ball? If he cannot spike well, it would be unwise for him to attempt this play. However, the good setter can also spike when necessary. In fact, on national teams you will seldom see a setter who does not have the ability to spike when necessary.

CONCLUSION

Basically, the purpose of the setter is to place the ball in a position from which the most effective spike can be made. Pass-set-spike should be considered as one continuing play, each equally necessary for a winning offense.

REFERENCES

1. Peck, W. H., personal correspondence, May 21, 1968.
2. Coleman, Jim, "The World's Cup," *International Volleyball Review*, March-April, 1966, p. 30.
3. Peck, *op cit.*
4. Scates, Allen E., personal correspondence, May 16, 1968.
5. DeGroot, E. B., Jr., personal correspondence, July 11, 1959.
6. Egstrom, Glen H., and Shaafsma, Frances, *Volleyball* (Dubuque, Iowa: Wm. C. Brown Company Publishers, 1966), p. 14.

---

7. Shondell, Donald S., personal correspondence, May 18, 1968.
8. *Ibid.*

See also the following references:

A. Coleman, Jim, "Coaches Corner," *International Volleyball Review*, March-April, 1966, p. 42.
B. Lowell, John C., "Thoughts on the Olympics," *International Volleyball Review*, January-February, 1969, p. 5.
C. Nemeth, Delphine, "Jane Ward Visits South Bend," *International Volleyball Review*, November-December, 1967, p. 15.

4. Techniques o
Spiking the Bal

By MARSHALL L. WALTERS and MICHAEL F. O'HA

THE English author, Peter Wardale, sets the tone for our chapter on t attack in volleyball, better known as the spike and sometimes referred as the kill:

> In every sport there is some aspect that has the spectators leapi from their seats—in soccer the centre forward jumping above t defence to head a goal from the winger's cross; in cricket the batsm hitting a towering six back over the bowler's head; in rugby a glorio passing movement which culminates in a try. So volleyball too has golden moment when the spiker, leaping high in the air, meets the s ball and smashes it into the opponents' court.[1]

It is important for any writer or any reader to realize that in sport the is never one "way to do it," or one way to coach, or to perform. Those wi wide experience and observation have seen champion athletes, in mar sports, break some of the "musts" of what many coaches teach as basi It is also important to understand that the views, the presentation, th principles of any one writer, or one school of thought, or one nation c not truly cover the possibilities of the subject.

The writers would hope that this presentation would be accepted a "some" views on the spike, with full knowledge that in sport there are n infallible absolutes. Nothing is "always" so, and there probably is no tim which is "never."

There have to be variations in spiking because the abilities of player vary, the type of team with whom one plays is not always the same, th opposition and its style of play changes, and the demands of coache differ.

HISTORY OF SPIKING

We have a game called volleyball being played around the world toda that is not *volley-ball*. The reason it is not *volley-ball* is due to the *spike*

which has come into common use in advanced play. It is an element intended to score for the attacking team. William Morgan, the inventor of volleyball, probably did not have this in mind when he took his two Holyoke, Massachusetts, YMCA teams over to Springfield College for an exhibition match early in 1896.

Americans have been proud of the fact that volleyball, now a worldwide sport, was invented in this country. It may come as a shock to those with a high degree of nationalism in their blood to learn that the spike, which revolutionized the game, was not an American invention.

Something new was added to volleyball by a backwoods team of the Philippines, who were the sensation of a tournament in Manila, by "hoisting the ball high into the air, near the net" and having a big rangy bushman run from center court and "slug the ball." No one could stop such an attack, nor could they find anything in the rules to prevent this method of scoring. So back to America came the news of "punching, slugging, whacking, thumping," or, if you like, "spiking" the ball.[2]

Today, for perhaps too many players, spiking means just one thing, and that is *power*. No one doubts the difficulty of coping with a real powerful spike, but the increased skill of the blockers over the years has cut down greatly on the point-scoring effectiveness of sheer power. ". . . it is not enough to be able to hit the ball every time with power; where you hit it is every bit as important if you are to derive the maximum benefit from the correct performance of the skill."[3]

REQUISITES OF THE GOOD SPIKER

There is no single physical description to fit the person who will become a good spiker. Generally speaking, the qualities would be much the same as those sought in a top-flight basketball player (i.e., height, jumping ability, good hand-to-eye coordination, and quickness, along with good conditioning and attitude).

It is safe to say that those who are overweight or who cannot jump high enough to get their wrist above the net, that those whose physical endurance is such that they tire quickly, that those who get easily upset at themselves or others, are unlikely to become successful in spiking a volleyball in competition.

HOW TO CONTACT THE BALL

Experts more or less agree that the ball is best spiked with the heel of the hand—that part between the wrist and a line drawn from the base of the thumb to that of the little finger. Preliminary to contacting the ball, the hand should be relaxed.

At the moment of contact with the ball, if the ball is to be driven downward into the court, the hand can be snapped from the wrist to give the

zip to the ball that is tantamount to the wrist snap of the golfer just as the club contacts the ball or of the baseball batter as he swishes his wrists into the swing. "This whipping action imparts considerable speed to the ball, which, coupled with the top spin and sharp downwards direction, makes it extremely difficult to handle."[4]

For a beginner it is well to hold the ball in one hand and slowly hit it out with the hitting hand to the wall or floor until he "feels the contact." By this is meant the awareness which develops in the neuromuscular system. From the standpoint of the philosophy of learning, it is the "feel

Fig. 3.   Direction of spike.

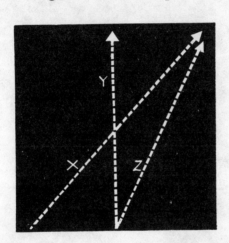

- - → Path of ball.

theory." All necessary parts of the organism have experienced or "felt" it, not once but many times, and it literally becomes *part of* the performer. He *knows* how and what he is doing and is confident of his movement.

WHERE TO CONTACT THE BALL

The spot at which the ball is hit by the hand and the angle from which it is hit will determine where the ball goes. Therefore, the principle of concentration must be applied vigorously as one learns to spike.

It takes little thinking to understand that, if the ball is contacted underneath or at a low point, the resulting impetus will deflect the ball upward in its flight. This will occur no matter what the angle of attack. By the same token, if the ball is hit behind and at dead center, it will fly on a

Brazilian woman player is in perfect position for the spike. Arm and hand are cocked behind her head ready to be thrust forward with a whipping action. U.S. blockers are caught unprepared.

straight course like a fast-ball pitch in baseball. This means that the application of some physics and geometry will be of assistance. The line of motion of the driving power must be from an angle above the back dead center of the ball, and it must be in the direction we want the ball to take.

68

The beginning spiker should practice first from a standing position. He should put the ball in the opposite-from-the-driving hand, hold it high as if on a golf tee, and then experiment driving it off the hand. He should watch carefully where the ball is hit, from what angle, and what happens to it on each drive. With the spiker standing about 12 feet from a wall, the ball should hit the floor about 2 or 3 feet from the wall, bounce against it, and rebound to him. Very strict attention should be given not only to the spot on the ball that is being hit but also to the direction of the course taken by the driving hand.

After the habit has been established, the spiker may then throw the ball up, or have someone else do it, and try to apply the same powerful drive. The next step is to take the ball to the net, use a take-off, and spike the ball into the opponents' court. This should be practiced first with the net at a height of 7 feet for men and 6 feet for women.

It is important again, at this point, to check the effectiveness of the hand, fingers, and wrist upon contacting the ball. Beginning spikers can improve their accuracy by hitting from the sides of the court rather than from the middle. As illustrated in Figure #3, the diagonal line X is longer than either lines Y or Z, so a ball spiked along line X has a better chance of landing in bounds than one hit along lines Y or Z. The diagonal spike also lessens the possibility of the hand contacting the net and makes it more difficult for the defensive players to move to the ball and block the spike.[5]

POSITION OF BALL AT CONTACT

Most players stand aghast when they see a small man spike the ball with more skill than some tall men. A little close attention and study will reveal that the secret is timing. In order to spike a ball successfully, it is only necessary that the ball be contacted a very short space above the top of the net. Contrary to some opinion, there is no hard and fast rule about height of the ball when contacted. Common sense shows the important matter to be that of the spiker and ball arriving at the same time some place above the net tape.

A *good* spiker should practice hitting the ball at various distances above the net. He should practice with setters to employ variety, with both high and low sets, and with sets straight up into the air as well as from various angles. Players will not reach their greatest potential as spikers as long as they insist on the prosaic 1-2-3 game, with the setter always near the net and setting the ball from the same angle all the time. Balls should be set from every possible direction, and the spiker should study his position and approach so he can hit from any of those angles. Most spikers, when trying these angle shots, crowd the ball too much. It is best to step back a step or two when attempting to hit a ball set from far across the court or from a front corner of the center-back position.

In this spiking action, Tom Haine, U.S. Pan American player from Hawaii, has already begun the downward thrust of his arm after cocking it behind his head.

POSITION OF BALL IN RELATION TO SHOULDER

Where should the ball be in relation to the driving shoulder? Much of bad spiking stems from not understanding the physics involved. The spiker needs to be aware of the fact that the ball should be lined up with the hitting shoulder. The ball should be out in front of the hitting shoulder and in a vertical axis with it. When the ball is directly over, or even back of the hitting shoulder, only an expert spiker can use enough wrist motion to get it down into the court.

It is possible to hit balls which are out of line with the hitting shoulder, but why make shots difficult? They can be made more easily and more effectively by cooperating with the laws of physics in applying the impetus. A piston head drives straight guided by the piston walls. If it develops a "slap" or gets out of line, power is lost. Therefore, a spiker should check carefully the spot at which he is hitting the ball in relation to his hitting shoulder. Again, this might be done more easily from a standing position, hitting the ball to the floor ahead and rebounding it off a wall.

POSITION OF BALL IN RELATION TO NET

The ball will not always be the same distance from the net when spiked. Some players do have a favorite distance at which they prefer the ball. It is best if spikers learn to hit the ball when it is directly over the net and at all variations of distance back away from the net. "On close to the net sets the ball should be hit with a cut swing, and on a deep set the ball should be hit with as much roll as possible, preferably toward the diagonal corner."[6]

Balls can even be spiked from as far back as ten feet from the net. This should be practiced by all players. The day for temperamental one-spot-for-a-set spikers has passed. Teammates do their best in trying to get the ball set for the spiker to hit to the best advantage of himself and his team. Therefore, the spiker has the responsibility of learning to hit the ball from any position when it is above the net. It is further the responsibility of the spiker to use judgment and not penalize his team, nor destroy the morale of the setter, by smashing the ball into the net when it should be played deep in the opponents' territory.

HOW TO TAKE OFF, HIT, AND LAND

It is difficult to spike the ball unless the hand gets higher than the net. All the hitting power in the world is to no avail if the following capacities are not present:

1. A relaxation, and yet a latent readiness to spring into any ball that can be hit, no matter where it is.

2. A spring upward with enough height to carry the spiker into a position to hit the ball into the opponents' court.

3. The training which gives reserve conditioning or endurance, thereby allowing the player to play through a complete tournament without undue fatigue or tightening.

While it is possible to spike from a standing position, in order to get maximum required height a spiker should take several steps. A lengthy run is hard to time and can often cause the spiker to touch the net or step over the center line.

The most common method of jumping in order to spike is the two-foot take-off. In the use of this method of take-off, the first requisite is development of enough speed, strength, and endurance in the muscles to get the body into the air high enough, often enough, and fast enough to meet the ball to be spiked. The above sounds pedantic, but it is surprising how many players have not learned these simple facts. Two or three well-timed steps, followed by a half step and crouching action, can put the spiker in position for his jump upwards. In teaching this procedure, we have found it helpful to have a student first take only one left step, close with his right foot, crouch, and then jump.

The matter of endurance really comes first, and many players overlook this fact. Toe bouncing, raising the heels, high rhythmical bouncing, high leaping, and other developmental exercising of this sort will furnish the muscle conditioning needed if they are done often enough, long enough, and regularly enough. Omission of any of the three latter factors will nullify the results. Isotonic exercise (weight lifting) is used by many of the championship players to increase their vertical jumping ability.*

Preliminary to the take-off, the spiker should have scanned the opponents' court to note the position of their players. This quick, conscious "photo" of the opponents and the spiker's position in relation to the net should precede his attention to the flight of the ball and the point at which he will contact it. The net, opponents, opposite court, and teammates will then become part of his peripheral vision.

The spiker needs to move smoothly and speedily to get into a position for the take-off so that his body will be behind the ball when it is hit. Many players take off from directly under or even ahead of the ball, and this is one of the main causes of failure to hit a ball correctly. Body position in relation to the ball is especially important on the "direct pass" or spike on the number two contact. Spikers at left or right forward position often fail to back up enough to be in behind the ball as it comes at an angle from some other position on their court.†

The amount of crouch preliminary to the take-off and the amount of squat or knee bend just before springing into the air is an individual matter. Some players seem to need little knee bending in order to get height. Experimentation by the player, with help from the coach, should determine

---

* See Chapter 7.

† When a right-handed spiker hits from the left-forward position, this is known as a strong-side or on-hand spike. When he hits from the right-forward position, this is a weak-side or off-hand spike. Championship players can hit almost as effectively from their weak side as from their strong side. The ideal would be for a spiker to be ambidextrous, but this seldom happens.

U.S. and Japan play before 7,000 spectators in Los Angeles. The spiker is All-American Al Scates, who became UCLA volleyball coach. His arm is fully extended to drive the ball downward. One Japanese blocker jumped too late to get high enough for his block. Jim Montague (No. 5), a five-time All-American, moves in to "cover the spike" in case blockers return the ball to his side.

this point. That style which fits the player's temperament and keeps him relaxed and alert, that style which gives ease of movement and a feeling of confidence, that style which allows him to move for a ball at any spot and from any direction, that style that gets him high enough to hit the ball well, is the best technique for *that* player.

73

The arms can assist in the take-off by giving lift to the body. This is done by raising the driving hand behind the head, as a catcher does in throwing to second base, and bringing the elbow above the shoulder. The opposite arm is raised quickly so that the forearm is across the chest. From this position the actual spike is executed by whipping the driving hand and arm forward in a short, chopping motion. McGown elaborates on this point as follows, "The actual hitting motion will be from a cocked position to a fully extended arm position as the arm provides a whipping, driving force. . . ."[7]

The spiker should strive to go up straight with his trunk erect and his weight centered over his feet. This causes him to come down straight and prevents his touching the net or landing across the center line.

In other words, the spiker's motion should have him contacting the ball above the spiking shoulder with the arm fully extended upward and slightly forward. Obviously, the ultimate spike is obtained by the spiker's being able to jump and reach high enough in the air to hit the ball over the block and into the opponents' back court. If a spiker is successful in accomplishing this basic type of attack, all the other spiking maneuvers (i.e., half spikes, "dinks," and cut shots) become far more effective, since the blockers will not know what to expect. The ability to hit any type of set quickly, cleverly, and with power makes a spiker of utmost value to his team.

A most important factor for spiking is the development of a "groove" for the spiker's spiking arm. In much the same way as a basketball player has a groove for his shooting action, the spiker needs to be able to swing at the ball with the same fast-stroking action every time. This type of continuity then allows him to use his brain, body, and wrist and fingers to determine where on the court he should direct his ball, as well as to decide at what velocity he will drive the ball. The quick wrist and fingers, plus a fast, grooved arm swing, allow a good spiker to hit even a bad set anywhere on the opponents' court. While each spiker has to select the groove that is most advantageous to him, the ultimate is felt by many to have the following characteristics:

1. The stroking of a fully extended arm, similar to hitting an overhead in tennis straight away, yields a maximum reach for a spiking motion.

2. If the same groove can be mastered as an effective motion for serving the ball, the ability to develop and maintain only one motion greatly simplifies the hand-to-eye coordination that is involved and thus tends to make both actions more effective.

STRATEGY IN SPIKING

C. C. Robbins of Chicago, who coached several national championship teams and was a former national YMCA chairman of volleyball, had a slogan which all spikers need to repeat to themselves: "A ball should

Marshall Lewis demonstrates how to "turn the ball down" in spiking by whipping wrist and fingers forward. This action was at a clinic conducted for U.S. Army personnel in Alaska. Clinic director, behind Lewis, is J. Edmund Welch, editor of this book.

75

never cross the net unless it is tagged with brains." His meaning is clear. Every ball hit should be for some purpose.

The real fun and stimulus in this game comes partly from the strategy of the spikers in trying to outwit the opponents by change of pace, change of direction, fake drives, pass-off plays, drop or "dink" shots, and deflection hitting. Strategic spiking requires the high set, the low set, the "Jap" set, the shoot set, the back set, the first-ball kill, the first-ball set and kill, and the first-ball set followed by a fake spike and relay set to another spiker.

Change of pace and direction is important in any game. A spiker who slugs away on all balls soon finds himself being blocked. Just as a fire-ball pitcher finds himself a victim of the opposition if he throws fast ones all the time, so a slug-spiker finds, against good teams, that the ball comes back as fast as he hits it. A moderately paced spike can be very difficult to block.

One should practice hitting at all speeds, using the same motion just as a good pitcher does. Such a varied speed in hitting is guaranteed to throw the blockers off and give them no set pattern for defense. Too few players can think and play at the same time, and, if the spiker makes the opponents use their intelligence on every play, he has them at a disadvantage. Many will then not be able to concentrate on the ball.

The "soft spike" over or around the blockers to vacant spots on the court can be effective strategy, provided the spiker does not commit the foul of throwing the ball. This is known as a "dink" shot, and it is an extremely important part of championship volleyball. A powerful spiker will fake a kill and then hit an easy ball right over or to the side of the blockers' hands. According to Lowell, approximately fifteen to twenty percent of the court is a minus area or one that is not covered. The spiker must learn the "minus zones" and hit his soft spikes accordingly.[8]

Wardale refers to the "dink" spike as the dump spike, and he presents an excellent description of its strategy.

> If the block is proving too effective the real answer is not to spike but to simulate the spike; then instead of being hit hard the ball should be gently tapped or dumped over the hands of the block with the heel of the hand, the stiffened fingers or the palm of the clenched fist into the inevitable gap behind. This play proves even more effective if the cover behind the block is relaxed or non-existent. Care should be taken to ensure that the ball is still cleanly hit and not carried on the dump and that the approach and jumping action suggest that the spiker is actually going to spike. Dumping is only effective when two or three opponents are made to attempt to block a ball which does not merit it. Moreover, if the action of the dump is kept identical with the action of the spike, the player can change his mind when in the air and really hit the ball hard if he sees that the opposition is not going to block, thinking that the spiker intends to dump.[9]

Even a mediocre spiker who uses intelligence with every spike finds that he can deflect the ball off the blockers' hands out of bounds or into the net. Again, a study of deflection angles will help if those angles are transposed to the net when spiking.

Teams should learn to hit the ball on the second contact. Also, if the first pass should not be hit, or if the opponents can be caught off stride by such a play, the spiker should be prepared and able to set the ball either from a position on the floor or while he is off the floor.

This idea of relay plays to other spikers opens the game to great potentials. Some teams are learning that power alone will not win important matches. They are learning that if the ball is moved to various positions at the net away from the concentration of the defense, many times the spiker does not need to pound the ball. Ty Cobb's old premise of "hit 'em where they ain't" is applicable to spiking in volleyball.

RECOVERY AND DEFENSE

Just as a pitcher cannot afford simply to throw the ball and relax and rest, relying on the infield to get all hit balls, so the spiker becomes a defensive player immediately after contacting the ball. If the spiker is being blocked, he must be ready to make a quick recovery shot. He must have both hands ready to pass or dig a ball upward before it hits the floor or to recover the ball out of the net. This skill comes only after intensive practice. Recovery shots are covered in detail in the chapter on defense.

GENERAL SKILLS

It is equally true that the spiker, to be of top value to his team, must also be as good as any other team member at serving, passing, and defensive play. Unfortunately, too many spikers spend most of their time in practicing pounding the ball, and very little attention is given to serving, ball handling, passing, and recovery shots. There is no place on today's basketball team for a "basket hanger" waiting for four other men to pass him the ball so he can shoot. There is no place on a volleyball team for the slugger-spiker who waits for five men to set the ball so he can smack it, sometimes in and sometimes out.

NEW DEVELOPMENTS

Recent changes in international and USVBA volleyball rules have forced a great change in the style of play. From a spiking viewpoint, since the opposing blockers are allowed to reach over the net as long as they do not touch the ball before the spiker does, the offense is normally forced to set the ball deeper in the court. This forces the spiker to become more versatile in the following ways:

1. He must be able to spike the ball well from deeper in his own court.

2. On a close set, he must be able to accelerate his approach in order to reach and put away the ball before the blockers can get to it.

3. He must be able to hit a "half-spike" (slower, relaxed motion) in order to throw off a stronger defense.

4. He must be able to "dink" the ball anywhere on the court.

Interpretation by officials now allows a spiker to use his fingers as long as a single, forward motion is employed. The "dink" shot can be used in the same manner that a pitcher uses a "slow ball pitch," to keep the opponent off balance and to force him to look for more than just a basic, hard-driven spike. Furthermore, points can be won by effective placement of the "dink." Even if a placement does not result in a point, it often disrupts the offensive timing of the opponents. They have to dig the ball, often making a weak return play. Lowell refers to this weak play as the "secondary effect of the soft spike." A weak return or "free ball" usually results in a winning spike on the succeeding play.[10]

The rule change granting the blockers the right to reach over the net has increased the effectiveness of the block. As the result of a better balance between offense and defense, the action is sustained as the ball is kept in the air for a longer period of time. Many feel that this in turn has created a brand of volleyball that has a greater crowd appeal.

TEAM PLAY AND MORALE

A team in volleyball is six players working together in a pattern that makes for smooth playing. It is not a collection of six individuals. Not only must the skill of the players blend into team play, but equally important (and some say even more important) is team morale, team spirit, or unified effort.

Any action by the spiker which will weaken that feeling of togetherness, of confidence in the team, is just as much a misplay as spiking the ball against the wall. Nothing helps the human spirit as does encouragement. Research in psychology has proven that beyond shadow of a doubt. The spiker is in a key spot to maintain high team spirit. He is the star of the offense, and he can make the offense click better by continually encouraging his setters. When a particularly good or difficult set is made to him, he should add real emphasis to his effort of encouraging the team.

In conclusion, we should add this note. Today volleyball has progressed to the point where a balanced team will mean that there are not three spikers and three setters, or four and two, or five and one. In order to develop a balanced team with the potential for many patterns of play, today's volleyball team should include six spikers who are also six passers.

This is presuming that we mean by "spiker" the "attack" man, or the player who attempts to make the scoring play against the opponents. With six men having the ability to propel the ball into the opponents' court, there is then in existence a *"volleyball team."*

The inference is clear. Everyone today must become a spiker as well as a passer.

REFERENCES

1. Wardale, Peter, *Volleyball: Skills and Tactics* (London: Faber and Faber Limited, 1964), p. 46.
2. Brown, Elwood S., "Volleyball in the Philippine Islands," *When Volleyball Began —An Olympic Sport*, pp. 88-89. (An article in the commemorative handbook, authorized by the U. S. Volleyball Association and edited by Harold T. Friermood, on the 50th anniversary of the publication of the first YMCA-NCAA sponsored Spalding Blue-Cover series *Volleyball Guide*. This publication contains the 1916 rules, the first rules printed in 1897, the articles of alliance between the YMCA and AAU, and selected highlights from the history of volleyball.) Available from USVBA Secretary, 224 East 47th Street, New York, New York.
3. Wardale, *op. cit.*, p. 55.
4. *Ibid.*, p. 48.
5. Odeneal, William T., "Offensive Volleyball," *Scholastic Coach*, November, 1954, pp. 38 and 58.
6. Odeneal, "Volleyball Tactics," *1958 Official Volleyball Guide* (Berne, Indiana: USVBA Printer), p. 135.
7. McGown, Carl M., ed., *It's Power Volleyball* (Pacific Palisades, California: P. O. Box 514, c/o Betty Ghormley, 1968), p. 6.
8. Lowell, John C., "The Secondary Effect of the Soft Spike," *1968 Official Volleyball Guide* (Berne, Indiana: USVBA Printer), p. 118.
9. Wardale, *op. cit.*, p. 50.
10. Lowell, *op. cit.*, p. 119.

See also the following references:

A. Baley, James A., "Teaching the Spike in Volleyball," *Journal of Health, Physical Education, Recreation*, November-December, 1964, pp. 57-58.
B. Cardinal, Charles H., "Teaching the Power Spike in Volleyball," *1967-1968 Canadian Volleyball Annual and Rule Book* (Scarborough, Ontario, Canada: CVA Publications), pp. 81-94.
C. Lowell, John C., "Techniques—Spiking in International Volleyball," *International Volleyball Review*, February-March, 1967, p. 13.
D. Lowell, "Volleyball Training Hints—Jump & Bump to Win," *International Volleyball Review*, December, 1965-January, 1966, p. 15.

5. Defense

By WILLIAM T. ODENEAL and J. EDMUND WELCH

A GOOD philosophy of volleyball is that a team is on defense whenever the ball is in the opponents' court. The key to winning volleyball is a sound defense which includes receiving the serve, covering the spiker, blocking, supporting the block, and digging the ball. It is difficult to separate the parts of a defensive system, for they go hand in hand.

DEFENSE—RECEIVING THE SERVE

Each play begins with the serve; thereafter, a defense should be built to defend against the opponent's serve. Each member of a team has individual characteristics which make him, or a combination of his abilities with others, more useful to the team against certain advantages possessed by the opponents. The opponents should be watched in other matches to discover their serving patterns, habits, and abilities. You may expect your opponents to ferret out your weaknesses and plan for their experts to serve to your weakest player, to your uncovered areas, or to players who switch positions. You should find out which opposing players serve deep, short, or to any area of the court, or have a tendency to hit the same serve every time. You may then play to arrange your strongest defense in such a way as to match your opponents' greatest serving threat.

Chart with your team the areas of the court and make specific assignments of areas for each player to cover on a serve defense. These assignments may vary as each rotation is made. The skilled and more aggressive player may cover a larger area than the less skilled.

There is no specific prescribed stance required, but it has been found that players can move more quickly when the stride stance is used and the knees are bent slightly. The arms of the player should be down, with the hands at knee level when making the double forearm pass. If the serve is soft or lobbed over the net, the arms are forward and the elbows bent so the palms face out directly in front of the face.

The positions of the defensive players vary, depending on the offensive

81

style of play your team wishes to employ, the style and effectiveness of the opponent's serve, and the ability of the players receiving the serve. If your team uses the 4-2 system of offense (four spikers, two setters) and all players are equally adept at receiving the serve, Figure #4 is employed. This is known as the crescent or half-moon receiving formation. It is advantageous to have a definite pattern of letting the front spikers take the outside and the back players take the center positions. When the setter begins in the left front or right front position, rather than the center front position, the formation of the other five players varies a bit from that shown in Figure #4, but, fundamentally, a similar staggered formation is utilized. Figure #5 shows the 5-1 system (five spikers, one setter). It

Fig. 4. Basic formation for receiving service when using 4-2 offense.

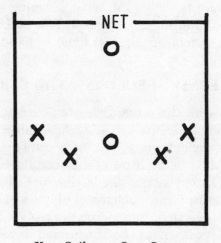

X — Spiker;   O — Setter.

would not matter from which position the setter originated. He would move to the center position as the ball was struck on the serve, and the responsibility for receiving the serve would rest with the remaining players. In Figure #6, or the 6-0 system (all players capable of spiking), any player could receive the serve. The pass goes to the center front position for the set. If the center front player receives the serve, the center back steps up to make the set.

As the diagrams indicate, the outside front players are approximately halfway deep in their court and the back players are halfway to three-fourths deep. The reason for this is that the greatest majority of serves land from the mid court to the end line. About seventy-five per cent of all serves will land within one step of where some receiving player is standing.

Fig. 5. Formation for receiving
service when using 5-1 offense.

Fig. 6. Formation for receiving
service when using 6-0 offense.

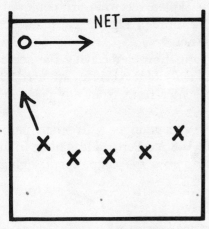

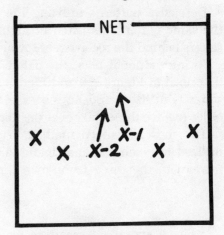

X — Spiker;   O — Setter;
⟶ Path of player.

X – 1 is center front;
X – 2 is center back.

If an opponent's style of service is soft, the defensive line-up may be
changed to Figure #7, utilizing any offensive style of play. Many girls'
and college teams use this defensive pattern.

If an opponent's style of service is hard, the defensive line-up may be
changed as shown in Figure #8. Only four receivers are used to receive

Fig. 7. Formation for receiving
service when service is soft.

Fig. 8. Formation for receiving
service when service is hard. X-1
is an alternate setter but becomes
a spiker if pass is directed to regular setter.

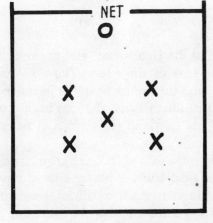

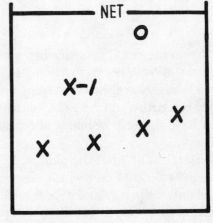

X — Player;   O — Setter.

the serve because it gives them more freedom of movement and access to the ball.

Defensive patterns utilizing the most skilled receivers are deployed in the same patterns as listed in Figure #4 through Figure #8, placing the setters behind the receivers or toward the net.

In international play, the defensive formation of receiving the serve is described in Figure #9 and Figure #10. Only four receivers are used. One setter is utilized, and he moves to the center front from any position in order to have three spikers at the net.

The most advanced method of serve reception is a five-man pattern utilized by such national teams as the U.S.A., Peru, and Cuba. In this formation, the three front men line up across the court about eighteen

Fig. 9 and 10. Formations for receiving service when using three-spiker offense.

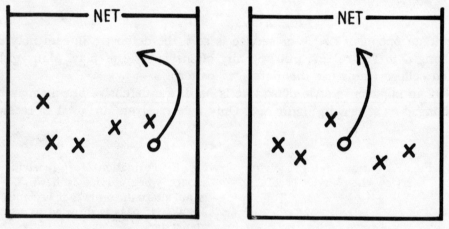

X — Spiker;   O — Setter;   ⟶ Path of player.

feet from the net. The setter hides behind the right front, and the remaining two players cover the holes in the rear of the court. The dominant serve receivers are the three front men, and they must be quick in order to cover the entire width of the court. On disputed balls, the two back-court men have the responsibility of "calling" as to which player should receive the serve.

Regardless of what the plan is, in the form of a shift or change in position, the rule is to receive the serve and then shift. A player should never move out of the way and expect a back player to get it. Likewise, he should not begin moving to his offensive position until he sees the reception of the serve.

In receiving the serve, the player should make every effort to get to the ball as quickly as possible and directly in its line of flight. It is difficult to make an accurate pass from an off-balance position. Body and court positions are the most important factors in defense. The players should concentrate on the flight of the ball and watch it come into the hands or forearms. In receiving a soft serve, the overhand pass may be used effectively. The player should let the ball come into the hands so the force of the serve flexes the wrists backward. With an extension of the arms and flexion of the wrists forward, the ball comes out of the hands in a high and accurate pass.

When receiving a hard serve, the player should be in a stride stance with knees flexed, weight on balls of feet, and hands joined together. The ball should be received in the knee area, and contact should be made with the inside, meaty area of both forearms. The elbows may be extended as contact is made, but the arms should move as a unit from the shoulders parallel to the floor and upward. The player should use maximum effort to get the ball in the air. "The tendency is . . . to initiate the movement of the ball upwards with the legs rather than the arms."[1] Many players cushion the hit by falling backward as contact is made. The body should be facing in the direction of the pass. Expert players adjust their arms to point in the direction of the pass when it is impossible for the body to be in this position.

DEFENSE—COVERING THE SPIKER

The purpose of serve reception is to pass a high, accurate ball to the setter. Just as soon as the setter sets to a spiker, the team should move into position to play the ball from a possible block by the opponents. As shown in Figure #11, the setter moves toward the inside of the spiker. The man directly behind the spiker moves to the outside of the spiker. The center back covers directly behind the spiker. The other two players swing toward the spiker and are responsible for the back court. All players should be alert, expecting the ball. They should think of the next play and know where and how to make the next play. At an Olympic development clinic held in 1967, Coach Donald Shondell of Ball State University summarized the task of covering the spiker, thereby defending against a blocked ball. "*All* players must be anticipating the angle of deflection. Stay low!"[2]

DEFENSE—BLOCKING THE BALL

The trend to International Rules has affected blocking techniques and strategy perhaps more than any other facet of volleyball. No longer may a back-court player come to the front line to block. This has ruled out four-man blocks and has made three-man blocks impractical, except in the case of an attack from the center.

On the other hand, blockers are now allowed to reach over the net, provided they do not touch the ball before the spiker hits it. This has increased the offensive power of blocking. Likewise, teams have become very proficient in keying a two-man block exactly on the spiker and, therefore, reducing the effectiveness of the power spike. The fact that only front-line players may block has resulted in a new emphasis on one-man blocks. There are more times now when a one-on-one situation develops.

Fig. 11. Covering behind the spiker.

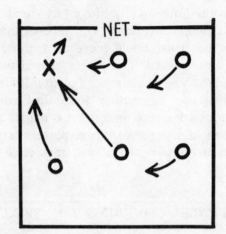

X — Spiker;   O — Setter;   ⟶ Path of player.

Low sets and shoot sets allow a spiker the chance to hit against only one blocker, but, surprisingly, many times this one blocker stops the spiker.

Effective blocking can be a great equalizer to a strong offensive team. The effectiveness of the block can be measured by the number of points won or lost through its use. However, a good block at a strategic point in a game is worth more than a point. The block affects individual and team morale. A spiker who is continually blocked effectively may lose his spirit, causing his entire team to react negatively. For the defense, this can give added inspiration and help make better team play. "Aggressive blocking will often offset aggressive hitting. The establishment of the aggressive attitude and performance of blockers often is the unrecognizable edge between victory and defeat."[3]

Techniques of blocking vary just as in any other skill of volleyball. However, the major features of modern blocking methods have been covered in an article by John C. Lowell in the *International Volleyball Review*. We have chosen to present the major parts of his article as follows

(Lowell uses two terms ,which may require an explanation. The verb, "stuff" means that the blockers push the ball down with a hard forward movement of the hands and/or arms. The noun "cripple," as applied to volleyball, is an awkward spike which the blockers can "stuff."):

The blockers must be constantly on the alert and seek every opportunity to "stuff" the ball into the spiker's face. European teams feel that fifty to fifty-five per cent of their scoring is done by the blockers!

   (1) *Ready position:* In this position, the two outside blockers must wait at the outer limits of the blocking area. This means they either block where they are or close together with the center man.* In no

Fig. 12. "Ready Position" of blockers.

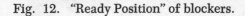

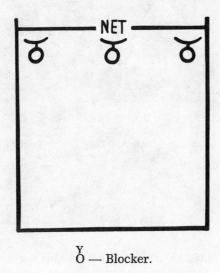

Y
O — Blocker.

case should the outer blockers need to move further toward the side line. If this is done, the center blocker will never have to "climb the back" of his outside blocker in an attempt to reach the ball. See Figure #12 for "ready position" of blockers.

   (2) *Individual Stance:* In this manner, the problem is one of keeping one's *nose in the net.* The blocker must never move back in order to get a better jump. He should stand close, with hands slightly above shoulder height and forearms parallel to the net. The forearms should be approximately 6 inches from the net.

---

* Good blocking strategy is to shift the biggest and best blocker on the front line to the center-front position, the next best to the right-front position, and the third best to the left-front position.

Larry Rundle executes an off-hand or weak-side spike at the 1967 Pan American Games. Argentina has put up a fine two-man block. Rundle was Most Valuable Player of the 1968 National Open Championships.

(3) *Lateral Movement:* All lateral movement must be done with a side step. A player should make every effort to avoid a cross-over step because he usually arrives at the block with his side turned towards the net. Lateral movement is keyed on anticipation and agility. A blocker should always try to maintain his "forearms on the net" whenever he moves!

(4) *The Jump:* The jump is made from the "ready stance," and the only arm movement is a simple dipping of the arms, still keeping forearms parallel to the net. A full arm swing (upward) as with spiking *must not* be employed. When a player uses the arm swing, it forces him back from the net and greatly reduces his effectiveness. A

player, to get the best block, should simply slide his forearms up the net till the blocking position is reached.

(5) *The Block:* The height of the block will vary with the spikers. However, the basic position of arms and hands remains the same. If the forearms are parallel and close together, this will insure the maximum possible blocking surface. The reaching over is done largely from the wrists.

(6) *Tactical Employment:* A block is designed to channel the hitters to an area where the back court players can defend, so it must be integrated with back court defensive positions. Generally speaking, the two-man block is employed so that the third man becomes a defensive player. The blockers usually split the ball on their inside hands. (This means the spiked ball will hit the left hand of the blocker on the right and the right hand of the blocker on the left.) When the attack is in the middle, the blocker on the side from which the set comes usually blocks with the center man. This allows the additional back court coverage needed against the soft shots. The three-man block is also employed, but it requires very alert back-court players. When the opponent hits (spikes) the second ball, all three blockers never converge on him as it leaves the defense wide open in the event he sets rather than spikes. The defensive team usually plays a one-two system with one man covering the hit and the other watching for a set.

(7) *Alertness:* Blockers must get high and be alert. Both blockers must jump together and come down together. At all times, they must be alert for a "cripple" which they can stuff down the attacker's throat.[4]

Since the three-spiker attack system is so common, the three defensive blockers must know how to cope with the options of this attack. See Figure #13 for options of the setter. He may make a back set to the right front

Fig. 13. Blocking formation against three-spiker attack system.

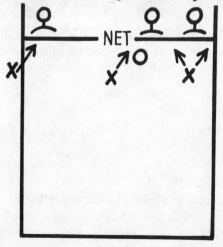

X — Spiker;   O — Other players; $\longrightarrow$ Path of player.

Blocking action is swift in the 1964 Olympic Volleyball trials. Player No. 29 moves rapidly to assist Player No. 63 in the block. Fast lateral movement is vital for the man who plays the center blocker position.

spiker, a direct low set to the center front spiker, or a regular or shoot set across to the left front spiker.

To defend against this offense, the two outside blockers key on the outside spikers and move with them. The center (best) blocker must stay with the setter and the center spiker. If the set is made to the outside, the center blocker moves out with the ball. If the set is made to the center, he tries to "stuff" the ball. If the set is made across to the left front, he moves as quickly as possible to aid the outside blocker.

Other important points concerning blocking include the following.

1.   All blockers *must* watch the setter. In a large number of cases, the direction of the set can be predicted. Once learned, this creates a great advantage to the blockers.

2.   Watch the angle of the spiker's body. Then shift your vision to his spiking hand to determine the direction of his hit.

3.   After going up to block, you must know how to move your hands quickly to the right or left to meet the ball. No longer is blocking a static, straightaway affair. Blockers must have good lateral and forward mobility of their hands.

4.   Blockers should not attempt to play the dink shot. This will be done by the player who is covering. (See Chapter 4 for a full explanation of the dink shot.)

5.   Recover quickly from a block and be ready to set or spike as the next play may require.

6.   "Blocking, while still considered the first line of defense in the co-ordinating defending patterns, is, more and more, assuming the characteristic of an offensive maneuver. Establishment of a reputation as a good blocking team can mean several points before the first serve."[5]

Building an effective and efficient blocking team depends on the principle underlying good team play. All players must cooperate, allowing each player to assume his full responsibility and taking over from another *only* when it will be to the team's advantage. Players must know the habits of their teammates and should utilize these to build good morale and a sound defense.

DEFENSE—SUPPORTING THE BLOCK

The two main defenses in supporting the block are known as the Man Back Defense and the Man Up Defense. These defenses are also referred to as the White Defense and the Red Defense, respectively. See Figure #14 and Figure #15.

The Man Back Defense is strong against power spikers and especially against spikers who can hit over the block, while the Man Up Defense is strong against the dink shot. According to Coach James Coleman of the U. S. Olympic Men's Team, the Man Back Defense is the best percentage defense. Actually, the top teams change quickly during play from one defense to the other to confuse the opponent and cause him to employ the wrong offensive tactic.

Another factor to consider is that the defensive moves of nonblocking players are tied into the strategy of the block. In a number of cases, the block is designed to force the spiker to hit in a certain direction where a defensive player waits to dig the ball up and start his team's offense. An example of this technique is when the blockers move slightly toward the center and give the spiker an opening "down the line." In this case, the defensive player is stationed right next to the line to dig the spike.

When the Man Up Defense is used, one back-line player is brought up behind the block to take all short shots and "dinks." He must duck to get out of the way of spikes which miss the block so back-court men may make the dig. The vulnerability of the "man up" to hard spikes is one of the main weaknesses in this defense. However, from his forward position, the "man up" is in an excellent position to set to any of the three spikers.

Fig. 14. Man Back (white) defense.   Fig. 15. Man Up (red) defense.

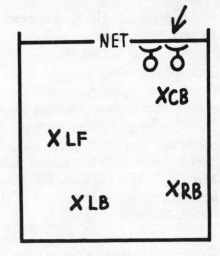

X — Defensive player;   X — Defensive player;

Y
O — Blocker;   - - → Path of ball.

Y
O — Blocker;   - - → Path of ball.

Since the Man Back Defense was the primary defense of the U. S. Men's Team which won the Pan American title, we shall present its details as provided by Coach Coleman. Refer again to Figure #14.

1. The function of the block is to *stuff* the ball *or* to make the spiker go cross court. Take away the spiker's power.

2. The Right Back should not have too much responsibility behind his position but is directed laterally and forward for the line shot, dinks, and balls off the block.

3. The Center Back should not have to worry about short dinks but he is more like a "free safety." He should be in line with the spiker and directly behind the block. He should get balls off the block, over the block, some

through the block, and long balls behind the Left Back and the Right Back. His moves should be predominately lateral moves.

4. The Left Back should see the ball at all times on the inside of the block. We are trying to force the spiker to hit to *him*. His moves are directed towards the ball with a minimum of lateral movement.

5. The Left Front should come off the net not more than eight to ten feet. He should be directed towards the ball and should not lean backwards or away from the ball. He should be especially ready for dinks.[6]

At the 1968 Volleyball Camp of the Columbus, Ohio, YMCA, Harlan Cohen presented excellent general guidelines for back-court defensive players. They are as follows:

1. Watch your opponents warm-up. This enables you to determine their best shots.

2. Watch your own blockers. This determines what position you take.

3. A short spiker usually hits down the line.

4. A tall spiker usually hits over the block and into the perimeter of the court.

5. When the ball is set back from the net, you can expect a spike deep into your court.

6. A right-hand spiker hitting on the right side of the court will usually spike down the line.

7. A right-hand spiker hitting to the left of the midline of his body will usually cut the ball to his left.

In utilizing defensive patterns, the top teams constantly shift their players during play. This is done to make the best of a player's defensive strength and to minimize his weakness. As mentioned previously, the best blocker on the front line is shifted to the center position at the net, and he is pitted against the strongest spiker of the opponent. Likewise, the weaker blockers are matched against the weaker spikers of the opposition.

In back-court defense the best digger is shifted to the center-back position. Usually, this best digger is a setter. The emphasis in back-court defensive play is to shift the players so that they perform from the same positions each time. This requires a player to concentrate on learning the intricacies of only one position. For example, the same player would shift to the left back position each time he is on the back line. Such shifting is not always possible, but this is the aim of well-coached teams.

DEFENSE—DIGGING THE BALL

Radical changes in blocking techniques during the past decade have been accompanied by new digging techniques. Ten years ago only a few top American players would "hit the floor" to retrieve a spike or placement by the opponent. Now all championship players will dive for the ball in order to make a "save." The dive is a fundamental that must be considered as an essential in competitive power volleyball.

If the diving action is to the front, it is followed by a slide of the player's body on the floor. The player then jumps quickly to his feet for the next play. If the diving action is to the right or left, the player continues his momentum and executes a side roll, often termed the "Jap" roll. Once again, his purpose is to get to his feet as quickly as possible after making the save. When a player digs the ball as the momentum of his body goes backwards, he will follow this action with a backward roll and come up to his feet, ready to play again. Wez Bridle, chairman of the 1967 Pan American Games Volleyball Championships, stressed the importance of the dive and roll in today's game. "You often have to dive to save a shot. You just can't skid. You learn to roll, get back on your feet in a split second."[7]

The dives and rolls increase what Lowell terms a player's "zone of effectiveness." This enables the player to recover offensive shots that he could never contact while still on his feet. According to Lowell, "With proper practice and training, a player can develop amazing ability to cover a wide horizontal area. Almost any player can expect to double and even treble his horizontal 'zone.' "[8]

In training the U. S. National Women's Team, Cohen has stressed that the players must go after *every* ball. This rigid training has resulted in Cohen's making this appraisal of his charges.

> "The women go after everything; hardly a ball hits the floor without one of the girls at least touching it. Maybe they don't save it, but they touch it. Next they'll be saving it."[9]

The back-court defensive player should be in a low, squatting position which enables him to "fire out," either forward or to one side. A ball in front of him will often require him to dive forward, bump the ball with a double forearm pass, and then hit the floor. In a rapid sequence, the player catches the weight of his body on his hands, arches his back, and lands on his chest and abdomen. By keeping his legs higher than his chest and by pushing forward with his hands, he is able to absorb the blow of landing with little shock to his body. Care is taken not to land on one's knees, but kneepads are an essential piece of equipment in both diving and rolling, as are long sleeve shirts.

Being able to dive laterally is important, yet the player should put his first emphasis on getting in front of the ball and using the double forearm pass to dig it. This is more effective than the single forearm pass or the use of one fist. For a ball to the right, the player should step way over with his right foot, pivot on this foot, dig the ball, sit down, and roll if necessary.

On very wide balls, the defensive player must dive out to one side, play the ball preferably with the inside of one forearm, hit the floor, and then roll. Although his arm is extended way out, he absorbs the shock of the fall on the fleshy parts of his leg, thigh, and shoulder and *not* on his knee and elbow.

Digging the ball by sending it high in the air is not sufficient. The player

Jack Henn (No. 22) is in a deep squat, prepared to "fire out" and dig the ball with a "dive and save." The game is between the U.S. and Holland.

must be able to dig the ball and *place* it. This is especially important in playing a ball off the block. That second ball, which may require a dig shot, must be set to the front line for a spike.

Although there are various ways of digging the ball, the use of the double forearm pass and the single forearm pass has come to be more

95

prominent because it affords more body surface for bumping the ball. It should be stated, however, that some players effectively use the closed fist, the heel of the hand, the wrists or wrist, and the back of the hand. On high balls, the overhand pass may be used, and this also constitutes a dig. Wilson made this point clear when he wrote:

> "We call the 'dig' any hard-driven spike that is brought up. In other words, a good digger is a man who can bring up a hard-driven spike regardless of whether he does it with a bump pass or with an overhand pass."[10]

The importance of the dig pass in modern volleyball cannot be over-emphasized. Thomas J. Watman, a successful high school coach in New Hampshire, stressed this technique as follows.

> ". . . we have found that the greatest single turning point in actual competition lies in the execution of the dig pass. While it may appear that this pass is primarily a defensive maneuver, its offensive importance cannot be minimized. Lack of ability to execute this play may result in almost complete disaster against a strong spiking team. If the players cannot execute the dig pass properly, they will find themselves constantly on the defensive. Sound execution of this play will result in turning point losers into winning points and side outs. From a psychological standpoint, the successful use of the dig pass can turn the tide in a close game. A team of strong spikers does not expect its offensive thrusts returned in an equally strong manner. When properly executed, the dig pass can force the opposition to alter its style of play."[11]

DEFENSE—NET RECOVERY

Another essential use of the dig pass is required for recovering the ball successfully when a teammate hits it into the net on the first or second hit. Fundamentals here are threefold. First, know your net. A ball striking near the cable at the top will drop almost straight down; a ball striking midway in the net will be pushed out by the recoiling net and will drop a foot or two out from the net; a ball striking near the rope through the bottom of the net will be held by the net and will be gently tossed or rebounded well out from the net before dropping. A player should experiment to become familiar with this pattern and know it well. Second, if the net recovery pass is only the second contact, then the ball should be dug back away from the net and high. This will guard against the common failure of hitting the ball back into the net and will also place the ball high where a teammate can be deliberate about spiking it or making a placement. If the net recovery pass constitutes the third hit, every effort must be made to dig the ball over the net. Third, by being alert to watch the ball strike the net, the net recovery-shot artist will move to the correct position, turn one

Barbara Perry, All-American, executes the "dive and save." After making the dig, she will do the "Jap" roll and come quickly to her feet, ready to play.

side toward the net, and, crouching, will wait until the ball has bounced as far from the net as possible before playing it. The possibility for him to make a good recovery pass increases as the distance between the net and the ball increases. Many net recoveries are made to look easy if the ball is allowed to drop almost to the floor before being played. This pause also gives the wise player more time to be ready to perform a good dig pass.

QUICKEN YOUR REACTIONS—HERE'S HOW

Playing a game in which at close range you must react to a ball traveling as fast as 67.7 miles per hour, you must seek to quicken your reactions. Train them to alert you to *move* to intercept the ball. Learn to time your dig pass so that a teammate may make a good set or spike.

Practice alone, digging the ball against a wall and keeping it up so it strikes the wall ten to fifteen feet above the floor. Use a variety of bump or dig passes as each successive rebound from the wall gives you opportunity. Emphasize meeting the ball squarely—practice—practice—keep digging it up—challenge yourself to count your digs until you can do so almost endlessly.

Practice with a partner. Toss the ball into the air so he may spike it *at* you. Have him spike it easily at first so you may employ your dig passes and may attempt to hit the ball back into the air toward him. He, in turn, may spike it again at you. This is practice for a spiker's timing; his spike should be directly at you, while your aim is to quicken your digging reactions. A net is not used in this practice.

Practice with a group in a circle warm-up exercise, using dig passes such as a pepper-drill in keeping the ball bouncing about the circle. In pregame warm-up while teammates are taking turns spiking, get them to spike directly at you and stand low in varying floor positions to attempt to use dig passes to field their spikes.

Set your personal goals high enough to really challenge your abilities. Then, practice—practice—practice to become a perfectionist.

REFERENCES

1. Wardale, Peter R., personal correspondence, March 7, 1968.
2. Shondell, Donald S., lecture at Olympic Development Clinic, Hawks Nest, West Virginia, December 2, 1967.
3. Unpublished notebook, Columbus YMCA Volleyball Camp, Bellefontaine, Ohio, June 14-16, 1968.
4. Lowell, John C., "International Blocking, An Offensive Weapon," *International Volleyball Review,* November-December, 1966, pp. 8-9.
5. Unpublished notebook, *op. cit.*
6. Coleman, James E., memorandum to candidates for the 1967 Pan American Games Men's Volleyball Team, May 9, 1967.
7. "Volleyball Slowly Gaining Fans' Interest," *Winnipeg Free Press,* July 20, 1967.
8. Lowell, "Increasing the Zone of Effectiveness," *International Volleyball Review,* November-December, 1966, p. 14.
9. Ronberg, Gary, "Playing It the Japanese Way," *Sports Illustrated,* June 5, 1967.
10. Wilson, Harry E., personal correspondence, October 9, 1967.
11. Watman, Thomas J., "Point Getting in Volleyball," *Athletic Journal,* January, 1965, p. 38.

See also the following references:

A. Alekseev, Evgueni, "Breaking the Defense," *International Volleyball Review,* April-May, 1968, pp. 46-47.

B. Keller, Val, *Point, Game, and Match!* (Hollywood, California: Creative Sports Books, P.O. Box 2244, 1968.)

C. Part III (Volleyball), *Proceedings, Fourth National Institute on Girls' Sports,* AAHPER, 1201 Sixteenth Street, N.W., Washington, D.C.

D. Whitehead, E., "Kaizuka Nichibo Women's Volleyball Team . . . 'Driven beyond Dignity,'" *Sports Illustrated,* March 16, 1964, p. 16.

E. Wilson, Harry E., "Fresno Wins National Men's Open Championships," *International Volleyball Review,* June-August, 1967, p. 59.

6. Offense

By WILLIAM T. ODENEAL and J. EDMUND WELCH

A TEAM is on the offense or attack whenever the ball is on their side of the net. Since only the serving team may score, a team is on the offensive when they serve, spike, or attempt to score a point or side-out with a volley.

There are several general principles which relate to team offense. First, all players must be skillful ball handlers. Regardless of the perfection of its planned system, a team that is not superior at ball handling cannot be consistently good on the attack. A team must spend the majority of its practice time in drilling for perfection on the all-important first pass and set. Second, a successful team depends on teamwork and coordination. Each player has a particular responsibility on every play and should not falter in his duty. All players on a championship team work as a unit and coordinate their duties with each other. Third, a good offense must be simple enough to minimize errors. When their offense is not working, many teams will change to an unorthodox, complicated system designed to deceive the opponents. Most of the time this newly devised system serves only to further disorganize the play, for it magnifies ball-handling weaknesses and results in more mistakes. Fourth, the style of offense used must be adapted to the team personnel.

In selecting an offense for a particular team, the following characteristics of the players must be considered: playing experience, ball-handling ability, height, speed, and determination or spirit. The key player in any offensive maneuver is the setter. He is the quaterback and playmaker, for he is called upon to make the perfect set to a particular spot where the opponents' block is the weakest. Often, he has to make the set from a difficult position.

BASIC SYSTEM OF PLAYS

A system of plays similar to those used in football is applicable in volleyball. See Figure #16.

The left front position is labeled Number 1, the center front is Number 2, and the right front position is Number 3. The opponent's court is divided into three long areas corresponding to the offensive front positions from left to right—1, 2, and 3. The defensive court is also numbered A for the front court and B for the back court. Before the serve, the playing captain calls every play and, if necessary, can change the call during a play.

If an 11 play is called, the left front spiker (Number 1) hits the ball

Fig. 16.   System of plays.[1]

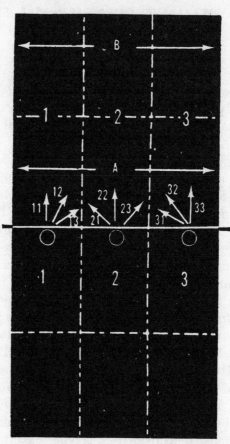

O — Player;   - - -→ Path of ball.

into the defensive 1 area. If the defense is blocking effectively, the 11 play is designed to allow the spiker to hit the ball off the outside blocker's hands or to cause the ball to miss the blockers entirely and land on the floor in the defensive 1 area. If this same spiker wants to hit diagonally across the court, the 12 play is called. If a 13 play is called, the left front spiker hits the ball sharply to his right into the defensive 3 area. Likewise, the center front man is Number 2, and he has a choice of hitting left for a 21 play, down the middle for a 22 play, and to the right for a 23 play. If a short dink spike just over the net is wanted, it is designated by adding the letter A to the number called. If a long dink spike to the rear of the court is desired, the letter B is added to the play called.

This system of plays can be basic to any style of offense and is adaptable to recreational or highly competitive volleyball. By using this system, every player knows who is to set the ball, who is to hit it, where it is supposed to go, and how to defend against it. Such a system gives each player a definite responsibility which he attempts to carry out, and it builds confidence in offensive play. Lastly, a system of plays strengthens team play and adds color to the offense, thereby boosting team morale.

The U. S. Pan American and Olympic Men's Team gears their offense to a code relating to the set. Sets are numbered as follows: 0 = normal set; 4 = shoot set; 3 = low set halfway between setter and spiker; 2 = low set in middle; and 1 = Jap set, which calls for split-second timing on the part of the spiker. He must hit the ball as it goes up out of the setter's hands. According to Coach James Coleman, a team does not score much by using the Jap set.

> "Its effectiveness is zero. Two times you spike the ball to the floor, and two times the opponents 'stuff' it on you. But you do *threaten*. You cause the center blocker on the opposite side to get off balance. Then your setter can set to another spiker."[2]

OFFENSIVE FORMATIONS

The Simple 6 Formation

Some women's teams and beginning scholastic and intercollegiate teams often use the simple six formation. This system utilizes the center front

Fig. 17. Simple 6 offense.

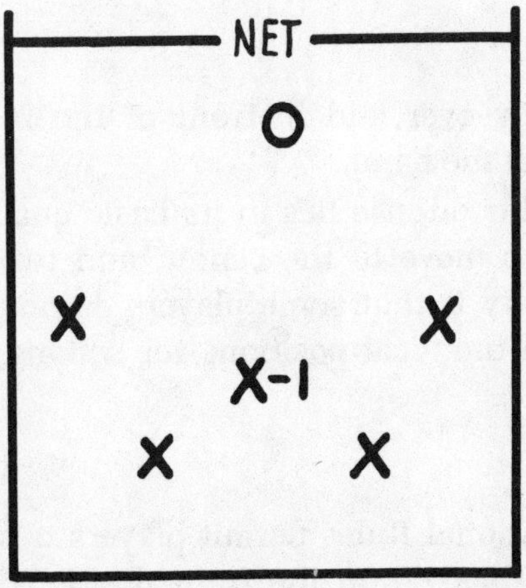

X — Spiker or receiver;   O — Setter.

103

player as the setter on every play. No switching of players from one position to another is done. When receiving the serve, the left front and right front players cover the outside lines, and the back line players cover the center areas as shown in Figure #17.

The center back is responsible for receiving short serves in the center and for setting the ball when another player is not able to pass the ball to the center front. The center back is also responsible for covering in back of either spiker. Most sets are made to the outside and about three feet from the net. The spikers attempt to vary their attack by using hits of different speeds, angles, and placements. They attempt to face the net on every hit,

Fig. 18. 4-2 offense when setter is in CF position. No switching is required.

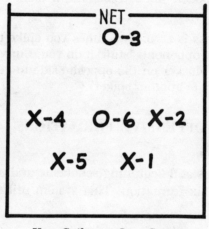

X — Spiker;   O — Setter.

hitting the ball directly over and in front of the face and changing the direction of the hit with the hand.

The advantage of this offense lies in its basic quality of simplicity. The setter does not have to move to the center, and two spikers are on each side. The main difficulty is that some players do not have the capacity to spike. They may be in the ideal positions for spiking, but they are unable to deliver a powerful hit.

The 4-2 Formation

USVBA and International Rules permit players to switch court positions after the serve. Strong spikers in the front positions may move from one position to another in order to give them more opportunities to spike most

Fig. 19. 4-2 offense showing setter in LF position and subsequent
switch of both setter and spiker.

Fig. 20. 4-2 offense showing setter in RF position and subsequent
switch of both setter and spiker.

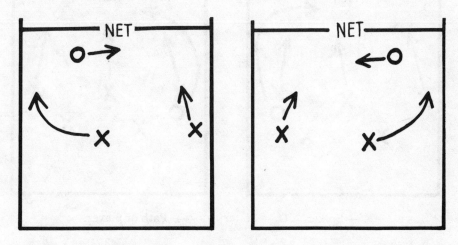

X — Spiker; O — Setter; ⟶ Path of player.

effectively. Many teams do not have personnel which are capable of both
setting and spiking from any position, and they need to rely on special
formations to suit the abilities of their players. Figure #18 illustrates the
basic line-up of one of these special formations—the 4-2 offensive system.

In this formation Player #6 is the best setter on the team, and Player
#3 is the second best setter. Player #5 is the best spiker on the team. The
other spikers according to effectiveness are #2, #4, and #1.

In this pattern a team will be making optimum use of its offensive power
on the net at all times. The two best spikers hit from the left forward
position (the strong side for a right-handed spiker) twice during the
complete rotation order, and the most proficient setter sets to the best spiker
twice. Also, this best setter plays next to the weakest spiker, thus strengthening his play.

With the 4-2 system, there are always one setter and two spikers at the
net. When the setter starts a play in the center front position as in Figure
#18, no switching of players is required. The pass is directed to the center
front, while the outside spikers are already in favorable positions. When
the setter occupies the left front or right front position, he switches to the
center front as the serve is made, and one spiker switches to the outside.
See Figure #19 and Figure #20.

The team knows to direct the pass to the center front position so the
setter may set to the spiker in front of him or behind him. Among the

Fig. 21. 5-1 offense showing shift of setter from RB position to front line.

Fig. 22. 5-1 offense showing shift of setter from LB position to front line.

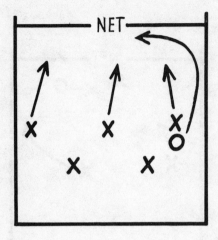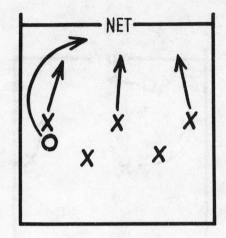

X — Spiker;   O — Setter;   ———→ Path of player.

several plays which may be worked from the 4-2 formation are the following: high sets directed to the sidelines, either forward or backward; low sets near the middle of the court, either forward or backward; deep sets to all spiking positions; and first pass sets from the back line to the spikers in the right and left front positions.

Until the swing toward International Rules a few years ago, the 4-2 system was by far the most common employed in the United States and Canada. This offense is still used to some extent by the major teams, but its most appropriate use would be by high school, college, YMCA, and club teams. The basic moves are relatively simple, and this cuts down on the possibility of errors. Coach Donald Shondell of Ball State University summed up the main advantages of the 4-2 system when he stated, "My feeling is, if you cut down the errors, any system will win. We are going basically with a 4-2 system. . . ."[3]

The 5-1 Formation

The 5-1 is an offensive formation which has five spikers and one setter. When the setter starts a play on the front line, his movements are the same as those in the 4-2 offense. He sets to the spiker who is in front of him or in back of him. If he occupies a back position, he moves up to the front line and sets to the left, center, or right front spiker. See Figure #21 and Figure #22. This three-spiker attack pattern can be used in the 5-1 system only 50 per cent of the time because the system is based on just one setter.

The objective of the 5-1 is to inject more deception into the attack than is possible with the 4-2 system. Along with this deception, the steadiness of the 4-2 system is retained half of the time. When three spikers are available, the center spiker is used many times as a decoy, with the set going to him often enough to keep the opposing blockers from keying on the other spikers. The low set is used, which also allows the center spiker an opportunity to hit the ball when his timing is right. The shoot set is made from the right center position over the center spiker and usually to the left front. All three spikers make their approach and are ready to hit the set, even jumping when there is no chance of hitting the ball. The center front spiker jumps as the ball leaves the setter's hands, while the outside spikers delay their jump. This makes for excellent faking and makes it difficult for the opponents to get more than two blockers up against the spike. In a number of cases, the three-spiker attack is so deceptive that the defense can get only one blocker up against the spike. This is the goal of a deceptive attack, for one spiker going against one blocker should be able to put the ball away most of the time.

A major weakness of the 5-1 system is that one man has to carry almost the entire burden of setting throughout a match. A truly great setter is required if this system is to succeed. Another weakness is that, when three spikers are hitting or faking, the offensive team is minus one man in covering the spike against the block.

The 6-0 Formation

The 6-0 formation is the most popular offense used in international competition and is destined to become the only pattern used by all major teams. Since the rules allow only the front positions to spike at the net, it

Fig. 23. 6-0 offense showing shift of primary setter from RB position to front line and position of alternate setter, 0-2.

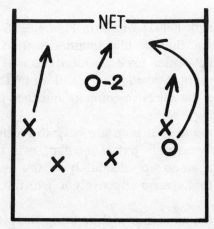

X — Spiker;   O — Setter;   ⟶ Path of player.

is imperative that all front-line players have the opportunity to hit in an offensive pattern. When the 6-0 system is used, the setter moves from any back position after the serve to the front line. The moves are similar to those used in the 5-1 formation. Actually, the 6-0 system cannot be employed unless all players are capable of setting and spiking at the championship level because this is what the code number "6-0" implies and requires.

There are several patterns utilized in moving the setter to the front position, but two of the most frequently used methods are shown in Figure #23 and Figure #24.

Fig. 24. 6-0 offense showing shift of primary setter from CB position to front line and position of alternate setter, 0-2.

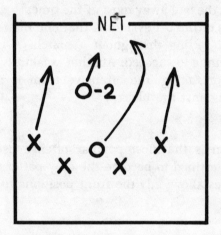

X — Spiker;   O — Setter;   ⟶ Path of player.

The player in the right back position in Figure #23 becomes the setter, and he moves in a somewhat circular manner to the front line. In Figure #24 the player in the center back position becomes the setter, and he moves directly to the center position to set. Both of these shifts have the advantage of allowing the setter to come in and face two spikers who are hitting from their strong side.

In both formations only four men are back to receive the serve. Player 0-2, who apparently seems to be out of the play, is in position to set when the first pass has not come up adequately to the center front position. Czechoslovakia used this system effectively to win the 1966 World Volleyball Championships.[4]

Most of the major teams do not wish to bring the setter in from the left back position, for this makes him have to set to two spikers hitting from their weak side. They solve the problem by using two players who are predominately spikers, two who are predominately setters, and two who double as spikers and setters. These last two are termed "technique players." When a primary setter is in the left back position, a technique player is in the right back position. The technique player takes over the responsibility of shifting to the front line and becoming the primary setter during this particular play. This allows the team to have two spikers hitting from their strong side.

We should like to add, however, that three national teams have used on occasions the left back player as their primary setter. The Japanese Men's Team did so in the 1966 World Championships,[5] as did the women's teams of the United States and Peru in the 1967 Pan American Championships. Furthermore, all of the major national teams have plays which call for sets to weak-side spikers. Their setters will not hesitate to face a weak-side spiker and set the ball to him. Likewise, when the setter faces a strong-side spiker, he will not hesitate to execute a back set to the weak-side spiker. Every play of this nature is designed to fool the blockers and give the spiker an extra advantage.

One of the most beautiful plays of the three-spiker attack occurs on a "free ball" play. A free ball is a weak return by the opponents. When this occurs, the already-designated setter moves swiftly from a back line position to the front line, thus putting the three-spiker attack system in action. The major teams are well-trained in this maneuver, and the players seldom make a mistake by colliding or suffering a mental lapse. The free ball represents an easy opportunity to put the ball away, so teams do all they can to capitalize on it.

Offensive Options

The variations relating to today's offenses are almost endless. We wish to close this chapter by presenting only some of the most spectacular options. To a large extent, these exciting options are standard procedures for the top teams.

1. The free ball is set immediately to the spiker, who hits away or jump sets to another spiker. At least one blocker must go up against the first spiker, or he will drive the ball down.

2. When a free ball goes to a corner spiker, he can fool the blockers with his jump set by directing the ball to a setter instead of to another spiker. This setter is capable of spiking and will usually put the ball away.

3. On a jump-set play when the blockers do go up, the spiker simply sets to another player.

4. The high-jumping spiker hits completely over the block.

5. The spiker hits a soft spike and causes the ball to dribble off the blockers' hands to the floor.

6. The setter fakes a low set to the center spiker and then back sets to

the spiker behind him. Likewise, he will fake the low set and then shoot set to the corner spiker. Once again, the blockers find it difficult to cope with a deceptive setter.

7. When blockers hesitate to go up on any spike, the spiker is quick to sense this and he drives the ball down hard.

8. The setter will move from the right back position to the right sideline. This puts three spikers in front of him for various sets.

9. The best setters can direct a back set over the head of the center spiker to the corner spiker furthest away from them.

Fig. 25. Two spikers split the setter for a quick option play.

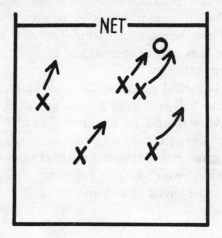

X — Spiker;   O — Setter;   ⟶ Path of player.

10. Expert players can perform these difficult sets while in the air—a low set and a back set. In addition, they have been known to set with one hand.

11. Two spikers will start on one side of a setter and then split him. The setter responds by using a low quick set so one of the spikers can get the ball down ahead of the block. See Figure #25 for this play.

CONCLUSION

The large number of options for the attack seem to give the offense a great advantage, an advantage so great that the defense would not have much of a chance. But one must remember that the rules now allow the blockers the right to reach over the net, and this is very much a compensating factor. Also, new defensive measures such as the dive and roll have tended to balance off the apparent advantages of the offense. The present volleyball rules provide a delicate equalization for both the offense and de- fense, and this creates an atmosphere for the most exciting matches ever played in the history of the sport.

REFERENCES

1. Odeneal, William T., "Offensive Volleyball," *Scholastic Coach*, November, 1954, p. 38.

2. Coleman, James E., lecture at Columbus YMCA Volleyball Camp, Bellefontaine, Ohio, June 15, 1968.

3. Shondell, Donald S., lecture at Olympic Development Clinic, Hawks Nest, West Virginia, December 2, 1967.

4. Wilson, Harry E., "Notes," *International Volleyball Review*, February-March, 1967, p. 32.

5. McGown, Carl M., "Reflections of a Journey," unpublished report of the 1966 World Volleyball Championships.

See also the following references:

A. Keller, Val, *Point, Game, and Match!* (Hollywood, California: Creative Sports Books, P. O. Box 2244, 1968.)

B. Part III (Volleyball), *Proceedings, Fourth National Institute on Girls Sports*, AAHPER, 1201 Sixteenth Street, N. W., Washington, D. C.

C. Scates, Allen, "Japanese Defeat U. S. in Pre-Olympic Exhibition," *International Volleyball Review*, January-February, 1969, p. 6.

7. Requirements and Preparation of Champion Volleyball Players

By JOHN C. LOWELL and J. EDMUND WELCH

MANY of the requirements necessary to become a champion volleyball player are similar to those required of the champion athlete in other sports. Likewise, training procedures for the top volleyball player are similar. In any championship sport involving prolonged jumping and quick movements, a high degree of physical fitness is required. In addition, the champion volleyball player, like the champion in football or baseball, must have a burning desire to excel. Nevertheless, there are some differences in the sport of volleyball which have affected the "requirements and preparation of champion volleyball players," and we wish to comment on these differences before developing the two main themes of this chapter, namely, "physical conditioning" and "intangible qualities."

First of all, championship volleyball, as compared to championship baseball, football, and basketball, is a comparatively new phenomenon in the sports world. The first national volleyball championship in the United States was played in 1922, but for many years the great majority of the teams had no formal coaching and did not undergo rigorous conditioning schedules. In fact, we can safely say that with the exception of a few leaders such as C. C. Robbins, Robert E. Laveaga, and A. Provost Idell, sophisticated volleyball coaching in the United States did not gain headway until after World War II. Only within the past decade have the best volleyball players been willing to subject themselves to disciplined and arduous training which is common to so many sports.

Our second qualification concerns the degree of teamwork required in volleyball. The highest degree of teamwork is essential in this game. A super star pitcher may carry his team to victory in a baseball game, but seldom can one super star spiker accomplish this in a volleyball match. All six players need to cooperate to gain the goal of victory. Minor morale problems are sometimes sufficient to wreck the best volleyball team.

THE IMPORTANCE OF PHYSICAL CONDITIONING

Good physical condition is the most important single factor in competitive sports. No matter how strong, how big, or how fast an athlete is, he is not going to succeed or be consistent unless he is in excellent physical condition.

Almost everyone has been blessed with an amazing gift—a body with no physical defects. However, very few persons, including athletes, study the body and work hard enough to even approach full development of their incredible physical potential. Physical educators generally agree that most persons develop their bodies to approximately twenty per cent of capacity, some to fifty per cent, very few to seventy-five per cent, and only the champions to a higher degree. This brings up the point that conditioning is a relative matter. It is important to be in good condition, but it is even more important to be in better condition than your opponent.

There is no easy way to attain this good conditioning. While only a few can ever hope to achieve the seventy-five per cent level, there is plenty of opportunity to surpass your opponents. All we have to do is *pay the price*. The basic components of a good conditioning program are as follows:

1. *Establish a routine to include plenty of sleep and rest*. It is, of course, far better to have a regular pattern of sleep. This will vary with individual needs and circumstances. When in a training camp, most European teams practice twice daily. They often take a short nap between sessions. On the day of a big evening match, they usually take a two or three-hour "siesta" to insure freshness.

2. *A well-rounded diet is essential*. We in America have all of the good food we need. There is little or no practical need for a special diet or supplements. If an athlete will eat three well-balanced meals a day and avoid between-meal snacks, he will have very few dietary problems.

   In addition, a player must keep constant check on his weight. There is no single factor that will destroy conditioning as fast as overweight. To achieve the best results, a player should stay in good condition on a year-round basis. Large fluctuations in weight during the off season result in a considerable delay in returning to playing shape. Also, the period of weakness, immediately following weight loss, will make the individual more injury prone until the body has a chance to revitalize itself. A player who cannot control his weight will never reach the top. There were *no* fat men on any of the teams at the 1966 World Championships in Prague.

3. *An organized routine of exercise must be followed.* The physiological problems are threefold. We wish to develop strength, endurance, and agility. In order to do this, we must first understand what each term means. Strength is the ability to exert pressure, and endurance is the ability to prolong this exertion. Agility is the ability to change directions rapidly.

To develop strength we deal with: (1) the contractile power of the tissue, (2) the physical levers involved in the movement, (3) the ability to coordinate all of the muscles involved in order to bring each into play at the most suitable moment. In order that both contractile power and coordination can be developed, it is necessary to perform a full range of motion when exercising. Perhaps the most suitable way to accomplish this is by using barbells in conjunction with actual play.

The most useful single exercise for the volleyball player is the full squat with weight on his shoulders. The full squat is not only an excellent strength developer but a *skill* that is vital to good volleyball. All of the good defensive floor play begins in a low position. If a player hopes to have the necessary agility to change directions in the low position, he must develop strength in this position. In addition, research has shown that the full squat is the best exercise for developing the principal jumping muscle groups—the quadriceps and hamstrings. To develop endurance, one need only increase the repetitions with the barbells. Exercising the upper body with barbells and calisthenics is also recommended. Particular attention should be given to strengthening the abdominal muscles which are vital to spiking. Running should be primarily sprints and explosive movements.

A RECOMMENDED EXERCISE PROGRAM FOR VOLLEYBALL PLAYERS

The championship player needs to work out three or four times weekly. This keeps the body tuned but allows enough days off to recuperate.

Exercise #1—Barbell full-squats. Start out with seventy to eighty pounds for fifty repetitions. A player should build to one hundred twenty to one hundred thirty pounds for fifty repetitions when he reaches his peak. Middle blockers may go considerably higher. If a player has a knee injury, he should be encouraged to squat for high repetitions without a barbell (one hundred fifty to two hundred repetitions).

Exercise #2—Using the stairways in a gymnasium or the steps in a stadium, have the players ascend by jumping up a step or two at a time with the feet together.

Exercise #3—Prepare a row of folding chairs. Space them about six to eight feet apart with the seat facing the player. Have the player leap over the chairs in rapid succession. A long piece of elastic can also be

Gayle Hunt, playing for the Kenneth Allen Co. of Chicago, shows the importance of agility and physical fitness in this unusual spiking action.

used to teach the players to jump. This is done by stretching the elastic in a zigzag pattern at varying heights from the floor and requiring the players to jump over it.

Exercise #4—Sprints. It is recommended that these sprints be limited to ten or fifteen yards. Eight or ten each practice should be adequate.

Exercise #5—Push-ups. Care must be taken to insure that the player places his hands directly under his shoulders and pushes up. When he comes back down, he should touch the floor with his chest, relax completely, and then push up again. If this procedure is not followed, the players will simply nod their heads and not develop their arms. Women should use the modified push-up on their knees.

Exercise #6—Abdominals. Abdominal curls should be used. In the curl the player lies on his back, feet flat on the floor, heels drawn in close to his buttocks, and then slowly curls to a sitting position. This exercise will be difficult at first but will pay great dividends in the long run.

This type of physical conditioning program cannot be followed by the athlete who lacks mental toughness and dedication. A well-known Japanese volleyball coach once stated, "No man can become a champion until he learns that his real opponent is not another man, but himself." One high school volleyball coach in Japan required his players to jump one thousand times each practice, reaching to the rim of the basket. Most of our athletes are not prepared to give their all in preparing for competition. In order to become a true champion, a player must learn to ignore soreness and discomfort, pass through the "pain barrier," and reach for his real physical potential. If, in his own heart, a player knows that he has paid the price to attain top condition, he will be a confident and greater athlete. He will know that he can handle any physical challenge that might confront him and have no regrets when the competition ends.

THE INTANGIBLE QUALITIES OF THE CHAMPION

We have stressed that a high degree of physical conditioning is essential for any player to become a champion. Likewise, the champion must have the physical skills to perform. But there are players who have possessed the required level of physical conditioning and the necessary athletic ability and yet have not become champions. What, then, separates the champion volleyball player and his team from the runner-up and the "also-ran"? These extra qualities are usually of an intangible nature. They involve spirit, morale, teamwork, purpose, and drive.

We asked competent observers to report on the 1967 and 1968 National Open Championships and to delineate these intangible qualities of the champion player and his team. A close study of their observations emphasizes the extreme importance of such qualities as spirit, morale, teamwork, purpose, and drive.

W. H. Peck, Secretary, U.S. Volleyball Association:

"I think that perhaps the most essential factor in the Fresno Volleyball Club's winning the 1967 Nationals was that of extreme team spirit, a desire to win, and a feeling that no one could beat them;

their spirit was always high and they gave the impression of being typical giant killers. Their defensive play was superb; their spiking throughout was adequate and at times superlative. The two big men, John Alstrom and Jon Stanley, frequently demonstrated ability to spike over blocks; their blocking was consistent. I guess in final appraisal you would have to say that the Fresno Volleyball Club was the most consistent team in the National Championships and that they very rarely lapsed into complacency which cost them a game or a match. They were an extremely exciting team to watch. The chief generator of spirit was Tom Bozigian, who was voted the 'Most Valuable Player' in the 1967 National Championships."[1]

Glen Davies, National Referee, USVBA, and International Arbitre, FIVB:

"What did Fesno do that the other teams did not do to win the 1967 Nationals? The answer is that they had three men to get hot at the right time, and they came through for them. Tom Bozigian hit from everywhere, and they were all good. George Serantos played defense à la Cohen and Engen in their prime. Len Kaczmarek had the two big boys, Jon Stanley and John Alstrom, 'pumped up,' and they kept bombing all night. It was just a case of wanting to win and going out and doing it. Fresno played better defense, and their block was much better than that of Sand and Sea (the runner-up). Man for man, Sand and Sea was much better, but Fresno had the better team on this night."[2]

G. R. "Jeep" McDonald, Member, U.S. Olympic Committee for Women's Volleyball:

"The truth of the matter is that I really do not know what Fresno Volleyball Club did better in the 1967 National Championships, except that a greater desire to win was their strongest asset. Fresno had two of the great blockers of our game today in John Alstrom and Jon Stanley, but Tom Bozigian had to be the difference in winning or losing the National Championship.

"It seems a little unfair to pinpoint *one* player's efforts in determining 'what a team did better' to win a volleyball title, but it turned out to be just the case as Fresno stormed past Sand and Sea in the double final. Bozigian was the psychological and physical sparkplug of the Fresno effort. Each of the players performed steadily, but it was Bozigian who directed and executed the great play.

"The title to Fresno was no freak. It was the result of the same characteristic of any championship squad; every player had a good tournament and a few had a great tournament. Fresno won the National Championship because they put everything together at the right time and the right place."[3]

Glen Davies, National Referee, USVBA, and International Arbitre, FIVB:

"There was nothing really different in the 1968 National Championships. Westside Jewish Community Center of Los Angeles simply jumped higher, spiked harder, dug better, out-finessed, and served better than Hawaii Outriggers, whom they beat in the finals, 15-5, 15-5. Blew them right off the court. Out-hustled them, also. Hawaii ran out of gas. The two big boys from Hawaii, Stanley and Alstrom, were stopped cold. They could not even 'dink" the ball against the Westside JCC defense.

"Larry Rundle got the Most Valuable Player Award. He was just as outstanding as he was in the 1967 Pan American Games."[4]

Harry E. Wilson, editor of *International Volleyball Review:*

"Almost all teams in the 1968 National Championships were coached *not* by a playing coach. The digging of hard-driven spikes with bump shots was good. The players on the better teams are not afraid to dive on the court, as they are now trained to do so. There were no big stars, but Pete Velasco and Jon Stanley are very fine players in any era."[5]

C. L. Bobb Miller, Chairman, Officials and Certification Committee, USVBA

"Blocking is the name of the game! All other things being equal, the team that blocked the better in the 1968 National Championships won the match.

"Attitude naturally plays a big part in winning, and the team that can overcome bad or seemingly bad calls by officials and linesmen, and shake it off, will be the winner.

"Conditioning is important, and 'Blood is the Badge of Courage.' "[6]

John C. Lowell, Manager, U.S. Men's Team, 1967 Pan American Games and 1968 Olympic Games:

"The first seven teams in the 1968 National Championships all played under formal, knowledgeable coaching. Reception (accuracy) and blocking were skills that separated winners from losers. Church College of Hawaii scored sixty-four per cent of its points on the block.

"Conditioning was another important factor. The teams at the top were ready to play forever. Church College played thirty-four games in three days!

" 'Deceptive' setting was not the premium that accuracy was. We beat Westside JCC in the National AAU with Ronnie Lang playing for Westside. In the National Open, when they took him out and put in a big blocker, they beat us!"[7]

Donald S. Shondell, Volleyball Coach, Ball State University:

"The winning teams in each division at the 1968 National Championships were greatly inspired and went all out on every play. Players on championship teams were in a ready position and *anticipated* each play. The top teams exhibited teamwork and team balance. These teams had a variety of men that could set and spike and had less tendency to specialize as setters or spikers. The better teams would vary their offensive attack, using fakes and 'pop' sets to loosen up the defense.

"Each of the championship teams had excellent blocking. The good blockers concentrated on their blocking efforts and took great pride in winning a point as a result of blocking the ball into the opponents' court.

"The outstanding teams never gave the opponents a 'free ball.' They would turn every deflection, every 'dug' spike into an offensive play.

"It was apparent to this observer that the competing teams were better skilled, better drilled, and better disciplined than ever before.

"The little man made his presence known, and, in almost every case, the big man was overshadowed by the little man.

"Defensive play was tremendous, and the top teams were consistently able to bring the first ball up to the setter. Serving aces and net serves were at a minimum. Among the final four or five teams, points were usually earned, and not given away by the opponent."[8]

Allen E. Scates, Volleyball Coach, University of California at Los Angeles:

"There was one outstanding team at the 1968 Nationals. The Westside JCC team that won was the best blocking team that has ever been put on the floor at a USVBA Nationals. Five of the starting six players had blocked together for two years, and there was no blocking weakness. The Hawaii Outriggers (the runner-up) had at least one weak blocker in the front line at all times. The strategy was simple. Westside set the spike in front of a weak blocker and then used him. Jon Stanley, who is the Outrigger star, had 6' 7" Tom Ryan on him in every hitting position. Outrigger came back the second game in the same rotation, thus enabling Westside to stack their best blockers on him again. Stanley had not seen a block like that since he played against Russia and could not adapt his shots. Prior to that match, he merely spiked the ball over the block and on the floor."[9]

Gene O. Chambliss, Assistant Coach, U.S. Women's Team, 1968 Olympic Games:

"The top teams were the top teams in 1968 for the same reason as teams were generally the top teams in the past. The top teams had a greater depth of good athletes. The athletes had a thorough knowledge of the game and the mental stability to carry out game plans as a team. Most of the players on the top (Open) teams had some international playing experience. Many players on the lower finishing teams were as good as the players on the top teams. Their team did not finish high because of the lack of depth in good athletes and mental stability. Also, the depth of volleyball competitive experience was not as deep on the lower finishing teams.

"Things are encouraging in that the depth of good teams with good athletes that have a better knowledge of the game and the mental stability to carry out game plans are noticeably increasing each year. A good example is that a top team of today cannot save its good players until late Friday or Saturday before they have to play them."[10]

Two of the most competent volleyball leaders in the United States, Harlan Cohen and G. R. "Jeep" McDonald, provided detailed analyses on the matter of championship players and teams. These are as follows.

Harlan Cohen, Coach, Westside JCC Men's Team, 1968 National Open Championships, and Coach, U.S. Women's Team, 1967 Pan American Games and 1968 Olympic Games:

"What do top teams and their players do to make them superior to the other teams and other players? The following outline, I hope, will answer this question.

Desire

"In order to be a top player on a top team, you must have the desire and interest to play volleyball. No one can force you to enjoy the sport of volleyball. It has to come from within. The players and teams which excel on the national and international level have a little more desire to train and play than the second-rate players and teams. However, when a natural athlete participates in this game such as Keith Erickson, who is naturally endowed with talent, he can lack the desire but still excel. I am thankful that these cases are rare.

Dedication

"I feel that this phase separates the men from the boys. Top athletes are usually the dedicated ones. The reason the U.S. Women's Team has improved so much over the past three years is that they had to dedicate themselves to training and conditioning and overhauling skills and techniques. Without this devotion on the part of the women, the past several years would have been wasted. The reason I have excelled as a coach over the last several years is the dedication I have had toward volleyball. Recently, my whole life has been dedicated to improve the women's play in this country. Many hours were labored over the study of films, interviews, international experience, and reading books.

Conditioning

"Volleyball players who condition on the beaches or in the weight room will usually succeed. Conditioning has been held uppermost in training the women for the Pan American Games. Volleyball and physical conditioning must parallel each other and not be separate. The reason the teams on the West Coast excel is due to the fact that they are in better condition by playing on the beaches and training with weights.

Competitiveness

"The top teams and players usually have that competitive spirit. Mike O'Hara typifies this perfectly. In his mind, he could not be beaten and usually wasn't.

Confidence

"Because of the domination of the West Coast teams, players have developed an air of confidence. When someone asks me about confidence, I re-

late this story that happened to me during the 1963 Pan American training period. At that time I was a player, and Harry Wilson was the coach.
One night Harry called us all in for a meeting. We talked about training
for the coming event and what was expected of us. He made one statement there that still sticks in my mind. He said, 'You are supposedly the
top players in the U.S. You would not be here unless you felt and had
the confidence in being the best.' Truer words were never spoken.

Organization

"To be associated with an organization such as the Hollywood YMCA or
Westside JCC where teams were coached, practices organized, and paper
work handled by competent nonplayers separates the winners from the
second raters. This was proved in 1967 when Sand and Sea lost the championship with all the top players because of poor organization, poor
conditioning on the part of the players, and lack of a nonplaying coach.
Harry Wilson and Sol Marshall proved to me the true benefits of being
organized.

"Volleyball in this country is progressing rapidly because of the five
points stated. I feel a program based on these will be a successful one."[11]

G. R. "Jeep" McDonald, Member, U.S. Olympic Games Committee for Wom-
en's Volleyball:

"The West Side Jewish Community Center of Los Angeles, under the
direction of Olympic Coach Harlan Cohen, made shambles of the 1968
USVBA National Championships by capturing the title with two consecu-
tive match victories over John Lowell's Honolulu, Hawaii, Outriggers.
Many common characteristics were evident in every team that survived
early tournament elimination and made a significant challenge for the
title. The purpose of this writing is to convey those 'ingredients of champions' displayed by every top club who made their mark in Portland.

"I attribute the success of any ball club to four categories:

(1) Leadership:

"Most other sports have more direct control over their athletes than volleyball. In order to accomplish the multitude of objectives necessary to
build a champion, one must acquire the primary ingredient—'*effective
leadership.*'

(A) "*Coach:* Unless we realize the value of a coach in comparison to the
value of a player, we will fail to build championship teams.

"Harlan Cohen of Westside; John Lowell of Hawaii; Val Keller of
Los Angeles; Jim Coleman of Chicago; Carl McGown of Church College, Hawaii; and Mark Watson of Columbus, Ohio, are just a few of
the prime examples of good coaching.

"McGown's Church College team finished in a tie for sixth in the
Open Division and pushed San Diego State to the limits in the Col-

legiate Division in their initial Nationals' debut. I might add that Mc-Gown spent two months in Poland last year with their National Team. Less than nine months later, obviously making good use of what he learned in Europe, McGown's squad pounded out significant achievements at Portland.

"Coaching is the volleyball team's pivot to success. Lack of it results in mediocre accomplishments. We had *good* teams that could have been *great* teams at the Nationals in Portland if they had had adequate coaching.

(B) *"Team Captain:* This job is second in importance only to the coach. Our failure to recognize this ingredient of a championship team will result in absolute failure.

"The captain is not necessarily the team's best or most popular player. His most important duty is to stabilize team emotion. He must have the ability to keep his fellow players intense. He is the floor leader. He controls the team while the match is in progress. He is *not* the coach, but rather he is a *coachable* athlete.

(2) *Sponsoring Organization:*

"I have always believed that teams derive much greater benefits if they are a part of a bona fide organization. The strength of support and purpose go a long way in creating the proper atmosphere for team and player development. A championship team and championship athletes must have a greater depth of achievement than being Number One. They must be prepared to carry out the responsibilities of that honor.

(3) *Program:*

"I am convinced that the 'ability gap' between East and West is mythical. I am further convinced that under the proper program of skills, practices, and physical development all teams are created equal. It's what they are doing that counts. The days of the weekend tournament player are over.

"From this day forth, any team or individual who wants to progress must work, work, work.

(A) *"Skills:* At least 2½ hours per practice session should be devoted to fundamental skills. All team members should be proficient in every area. The day of hiding a player is over. We must produce the *complete* volleyball player. Use creative and imaginative drills for good practice sessions.

(B) *"Conditioning:* We must challenge the physical durability of every player. The bloody arm or leg is a mark of achievement; the lily-white unmarked body is a mark of laziness. Players should leave the weekly practice sessions completely exhausted. *The More Intense the Program, the More Effective the Results.*

(4) *Player Talent:*

"Basic talent must be available to produce championship teams. Let's consider several aspects of the complete player.

(A) "He must have good lateral movement.

(B) "He must have good vertical jump.

(C) "He must have excellent court sense.

(D) "He must be involved in the complete team effort.

(E) "He must be *intense*.

"Westside JCC and many of the contenders had the aforementioned ingredients. The degree to which they performed at Portland was relative to the strength they possessed in each of the four categories—*Leadership, Sponsoring Organization, Program,* and *Player Talent.* You, too, can build a winning team by following the lead of these championship clubs."[12]

REFERENCES

1. Peck, W. H., personal correspondence, August 9, 1967.
2. Davies, Glen, personal correspondence, August 16, 1967.
3. McDonald, G. R., personal correspondence, August 21, 1967.
4. Davies, personal correspondence, May 14, 1968.
5. Wilson, Harry E., personal correspondence, May 15, 1968.
6. Miller, C. L. Bobb, personal correspondence, May 16, 1968.
7. Lowell, John C., personal correspondence, May 15, 1968.
8. Shondell, Donald S., personal correspondence, May 18, 1968.
9. Scates, Allen E., personal correspondence, May 15, 1968.
10. Chambliss, Gene O., personal correspondence, May 21, 1968.
11. Cohen, Harlan, personal correspondence, May 18, 1968.
12. McDonald, G. R., personal correspondence, May 19, 1968.

See also the following references:

A. "An Interview With Vaclav Matiasek," *International Volleyball Review,* June-August, 1968, pp. 67-68.

B. Boslooper, Thomas, "The Ideal Woman: Fit and Feminine," *Journal of Physical Education,* March-April, 1968, pp. 99-102.

C. Coleman, Jim, "USSR vs USA in Canada," *International Volleyball Review,* December, 1965-January, 1966, pp. 5-6.

D. Crockett, P. A., Plotnicki, B. A., and Medlin, C. H., Jr., "A Study of Physiological Aspects in Volleyball Players Before and After a Prolonged Period of Participation," *1965 Official Volleyball Guide* (Berne, Indiana: USVBA Printer), pp. 112-113.

E. Eggert, Del, "Conditioning for Volleyball," *1966 Official Volleyball Guide* (Berne, Indiana: USVBA Printer), pp. 109-110.

F. Layman, Richard, "The Most Abused Exercise" (deep knee bend), *Journal of Physical Education,* November-December, 1964, pp. 41-42.

G. Lowell, John C., "Jump Training Outline," *International Volleyball Review,* November-December, 1967, p. 9.

H. Lowell, "Fundamentals & Statistics," *International Volleyball Review,* June-August, 1968, p. 64.

I. Lowell, "Pre-Olympic Trial Conditioning," *International Volleyball Review*, April-May, 1968, p. 43.

J. Lowell, "U. S. Men's Volleyball Team Wins Pan Am Title," *International Volleyball Review*, November-December, 1967, p. 4.

K. Lowell, "Volleyball Training Hints—Jump & Bump to Win," *International Volleyball Review*, December, 1965-January, 1966, pp. 15-16.

L. Marshall, Sol H., "Colleges Hold Key to U. S. Volleyball Success," *Amateur Athlete*, May, 1967, pp. 16, 37.

M. McVicar, J. W., "Fitness in Volleyball," *Journal of Physical Education*, July-August, 1962, pp. 131-132.

N. Mott, Jane A., *Conditioning for Women* (Dubuque, Iowa: Wm. C. Brown Company Publishers, 1966).

O. Otott, Major George E., "Circuit (Power) Training," *Sport International*, No. 35/E, 1967, pp. 14-21. Available from CISM, 119, avenue Franklin Roosevelt, Brussels 5, Belgium.

P. Ricci, Benjamin, *Physical &Physiological Conditioning for Men* (Dubuque, Iowa: Wm. C. Brown Company Publishers, 1966).

Q. Ryan, Allan J., "Smoking and Health," *Journal of the Canadian Association for Health, Physical Education, and Recreation*, April-May, 1967, pp. 32-33.

R. Scates, Allen E., "A Participating Player's Observations of the World Championships," *International Volleyball Review*, November-December, 1966, pp. 6-7.

S. Shondell, Donald S., "The Relationship of Selected Motor and Anthropometric Traits to Successful Volleyball Performance" (unpublished P.E.D. dissertation, Indiana University, Bloomington, Indiana, 1969).

T. Tiidus, Arvo, "The Physical Fitness Status of the Canadian 1959 and 1963 Pan American Volleyball Teams" (unpublished M.S. thesis, University of Illinois, Champaign, Illinois, 1964).

8. Officiating

By E. DOUGLAS BOYDEN

ANY treatment of volleyball officiating must take into account the three main administrative bodies concerning this sport. This chapter stresses officiating techniques of the United States Volleyball Association, with a short concluding section pertaining to methods employed by the International Volleyball Federation. Officiating references concerning the third administrative body, the Division for Girls' and Women's Sports of the American Association for Health, Physical Education, and Recreation, may be found in Chapter 10.

In every sport the officials are an important part of the game. Upon their judgment, many times, rests the outcome of the game or match. Volleyball is no exception to this rule. Having alert, decisive, and discerning officials can make the difference between a good or poor tournament.

Being a volleyball official is difficult, but, as in every other sport, the official is an important part of the game. If the game of volleyball is to continue to grow and develop, there must be those who are willing and competent to officiate and guide it in its growth. There is a good bit of educating to be done with the general public and with many players relative to what constitutes good officiating.

Some might ask why volleyball is so difficult to officiate. When one considers that a spiked ball travels up to 67.7 miles per hour and the official must determine how the ball is played by the defensive team, it is easy to see the importance of having competent officials.[1] An official must be "on his toes" at all times to render the best decisions possible, not only on spiked balls but for all kinds of court play.

The English author, Peter Wardale, sums up the referee's plight as follows:

> ". . . there is a tremendous feeling of exposure when refereeing a match. The referee stands or sits on a platform overlooking the net, the court, and the players. From this Olympian height he controls the game and if he boobs on a decision it is an awful long way for the

ground to swallow him up. At least in some other sports the referee can run away to another part of the field or court!"[2]

In addition to being an individual who can make instantaneous decisions, the official must also be a student of the rules. It is quite possible for an official to make a mistake in judgment, but he should never make a mistake in rules interpretation. It is highly recommended that an official study the rules carefully before each match or tournament unless he officiates very regularly. This gives him an opportunity to "sharpen up" before the contest. Conferences or "warm-up sessions" of tournament officials prior to matches also help alert all to specific rules and help assure uniformity of interpretations.

There are at least six officials who must be considered as being very important to the success of a volleyball game: referee, umpire, scorer, timekeeper, and at least two linesmen. Each of these officials has a number of very important duties to perform if the outcome of the game is to be satisfactorily achieved. Although all of the above-mentioned officials are important, "the referee shall be the superior official of the game and shall have the power to overrule decisions of other officials when, in his opinion, they have made fouls."[3]

Probably the greatest problem confronting the referee is the consistency with which he calls fouls. Volleyball is probably the most difficult game to referee, since the ball may not come to rest for a period of time. It may not be held, carried, or thrown, as in most other sports. It must be "clearly hit." This means there cannot be any visible follow-through to speak of, or the ball is considered to be carried, lifted, or thrown. Therefore, one referee may see a play somewhat differently from another. The particular angle at which a referee sees the play can also make a difference. As for the spectators, who may or may not know the rules, they may cause the unseasoned referee concern when they vent their response to a called or uncalled play.

CONSISTENCY AND STANDARDIZATION

Since this problem of ball handling seems to be the major difficulty in refereeing, let us look into some of the points that might help toward better consistency and standardization in calling.

First of all, consider playing the ball with open palms in the underhand position. The rule specifies that "the ball must be clearly hit." "We know that a ball which makes a complete change in direction *must* physically come to a stop at the point where its forward force is overcome by a stronger force sending it back the way it came. Knowing the ball must come to a stop, it cannot be ruled that it must not stop. What margin of stopping do we allow? The rule says the player commits a foul when (in the opinion of the proper official) the ball *visibly* comes to rest at contact. This means that the open palm play is legal if the ball does not *visibly*

Referee watches action from a stable and comfortable platform, an
essential for good officiating.

come to rest against that palm. Nothing is said about sound or lack of sound. The rule does not mention senses other than sight. The judgment must be based upon the visual sense only. However, it is commonly known that a player is most likely to allow the ball to come to rest visibly if he plays it with the palms of two hands underhand, from behind the shoulder, from behind his head, or overhead with his back to the net."[4]

This official rules interpretation stresses an official should be sure that he *sees* the ball come to rest. If he is not sure, he should not call a foul. Also, he should never anticipate a foul. He should wait until it happens and then call it. It should also be kept in mind that in no place in the rules, except in serving, does it state a ball must be played with the fist, heel of hand, back of hand, or forearm to be legal. It is realized that if it is played in one of these ways, it will probably be a cleaner played ball.

The set is another one of the problems. If the ball visibly comes to rest while a player is setting, then it is a foul. However, an official should not assume, anticipate, or "think" it came to rest. The referee should know by seeing or he should not call it.

The same is true of the spike. A spiker may hit the ball on the palm without throwing it or changing the direction of the ball. When he hits in this fashion, it may make a loud noise. This does not mean it is a foul. A player using his palm to spike the ball is more apt to throw it than a player who uses the heel of his hand or his fist, but, again, the referee should not anticipate or guess. If he is not sure, he should not call it. In recent years we have seen spikers develop the skill of soft spiking with the fingers and yet not throw the ball.

Receiving the serve causes difficulty also. If a server serves a ball that is wobbling, it is quite possible for the receiver to make a double contact; however, the referee should be sure of this before calling it. On the other hand, if the ball does not come out of the receiver's hands in a perfect pass, it does not mean the receiver carried, lifted, or double-contacted the ball. On many serves a ball is not played properly and comes off the player's fingers or palms "dead." If the player did not hold or lift the ball, this is simply a poorly played ball and should not be called. Here again, the referee must know the difference between holding, lifting, carrying, and misplayed balls.

The same is true of a hard-driven spike. On a hard-driven spike, the rules state that a player may make successive contacts if they constitute one attempt to play the ball. Therefore, if a player gets in front of one of these hard-driven spikes and gets his hand or hands on the ball and his reaction time is off because of the impact of the spike, it should not be called a lift or carry. The player, in this case, should be given credit for judging and contacting the ball, and his performance should be considered as one attempt to play it.

Many referees get themselves into difficulty because they are too strict. They tend to anticipate. They call some fouls and not others because the plays are borderline cases. This is inconsistent calling and gets the official into difficulty with the players. If a foul is made, it should be called. On the other hand, if there is a question, by all means give the benefit to the player. Always remember that the prime reason for an official in any game is to help the players have a better and fairer game. He is present only to help the game and not to make a spectacle of himself by seeing how often he can blow the whistle, thus giving the impression that "I am a tough referee" or "I am the king-pin in this contest."

According to Wardale, "The Referee is not a dictator and the players are not playing for his benefit. It is rather the other way round. The acid test is to ask the question 'did the game improve through this official's administration?'"[5]

GOOD PRACTICES

There are a number of good practices which might be thought of as "Marks of a Good Volleyball Official." If an official can master these ten practices, he will, in all probability, be a top official:

1. *Friendly attitude.* He should always maintain a friendly attitude toward the players. In the carrying out of his duties, it should be done in a professional rather than an authoritative manner. A friendly smile can be helpful.

2. *Fair and firm decisions.* He should be sure that his decisions are impartial at all times. If a mistake is made, he should not be afraid to change his decision. However, this should be the exception, and his decisions when made must be firm. These actions will instill confidence in both teams.

3. *Expert knowledge of rules.* The official should know and be able to interpret the playing rules. This will give the players confidence and will ease tension. He should notify the player or players immediately upon the infraction of the rules. Players should not be left to wonder what happened.

4. *Positive whistle.* He should keep his whistle in his mouth while the ball is in play. His decisions or calls should be made quickly and sharply following an infraction of the rules. A slow whistle puts doubt in the minds of the players and spectators. "Excessive use of the whistle such as getting the attention of the scorer, captains, or umpire should not be used."[6]

5. *Instant hand signals.* He should use the official hand signals immediately after calling a violation. Such signals should be executed in a decisive manner but without exhibitionism.

6. *Controlled emotions.* He should keep his emotions under control, no matter what the situation. Except in very unusual situations, he should **not** leave the official's stand during a game. If need be, he should

VOLLEYBALL
OFFICIAL
HAND SIGNALS

HAND OVER NET
Stretch hand over the net from the side of the offending team.

SIDE OUT
Stretch out arm horizontally to the side which is to serve.

CONTACTING NET
Touch net and point to the offending player.

POINT
Raise index finger and arm on the side of the team which scores the point.

CROSSING CENTRE OR ATTACK LINE
Point to foot on the offending side and point to player.

DOUBLE FAULT
Raise arms shoulder height and hold up the thumbs.

OUT OF POSITION
Move hand back and forth in a sweeping motion.

DOUBLE HIT
Hold up two fingers to the side of the offending player's team.

TIME — OUT
Form a "T" with the hand on the side requesting time-out.

LIFTED BALL
One or two hands are raised with palms upward.

SUBSTITUTION
Move hands in circular motion and point to team requesting the substitution.

FOUR HITS
Hold up four fingers to the side of the offending team.

END OF MATCH
Cross arms at chest.

Used by permission from the *Official Volleyball Program*, 5th Pan American Games, Winnipeg, Canada, 1967.

call a player to the stand to interpret. If it is necessary to dismiss a player from the game, it should be done in an inconspicuous manner after an explanation to the player and the coach. If it is necessary to interpret between two teams, the referee should call the captains of both teams together and explain his decision to them. "Remember . . . that the captains have the right to speak to you about the rules and you must handle them tactfully and courteously."[7]

7. *Neat appearance.* He should always wear the official uniform. It should be neat and clean. He should stand in an erect position.

8. *Sound judgment.* It is imperative that the official be a clear thinker with sound judgment. The noise of the players or spectators should not sway his thinking.

9. *Consistent calling.* He should be able to maintain a consistent level of officiating through a match. Therefore, it is necessary that an official know what he is calling and why.

10. *Punctuality.* He should be ready to officiate fifteen minutes before the scheduled time, and he should see that all games start on time. Many tournaments run too long because the officials do not stick to the tournament time schedule. This is inexcusable and has many bad effects on the tournament.

During the course of a tournament, it is possible that another official or player may question an official's ability due to a decision that was or was not rendered. It is considered sound professional ethics for officials not to discuss one another's decisions openly. If an official has a question about another's decision or call, it is good practice to speak to the official involved when he is alone to secure his interpretation or to consult the chairman of the officials.

As mentioned in the "Marks of a Good Official," all officials should use the official hand signals properly so that the scorer, the players, and the spectators know which rule has been violated.

Keeping track of the serving team is another responsibility of the referee. He may ask the umpire to assist him, but he should keep track of the service himself. Numerous devices are used. Here are several suggestions which have proven satisfactory:

1. The referee puts his hand on top of the net nearest the team that is serving. When it is side out, he changes the hand.

2. A towel or handkerchief is tied to the top end of the net. If the team to the left of the referee is serving, the towel is hung over the left side of the net. If the team on the right is serving, the towel is hung over the right side.

3. The left hand and left foot are forward if the team on the left side of the referee is serving, and the right hand and right foot are forward if the right team is serving.

OFFICIAL **VOLLEYBALL** SCORE SHEET
AND GAME RECORD
Approved by the Canadian Volleyball Association

Name of tournament:
Type of competition:
Place – Gym. :

Date of play:
Scheduled starting time for match:
Time of start: Time of finish:

Name of Team (A) :

Names of players	Shirt No	Game 1. Line Sub.	Game 2. Line Sub.	Game 3. Line Sub.	Game 4. Line Sub.	Game 5. Line Sub.

Court Positions	Game 1. Line Sub.	Game 2. Line Sub.	Game 3. Line Sub.	Game 4. Line Sub.	Game 5. Line Sub.
(1) Back R.					
(2) Front R.					
(3) Front C.					
(4) Front L.					
(5) Back L.					
(6) Back C.					

Name of Captain:
Name of Coach :

Name of Team (B) :

Names of players	Shirt No	Game 1. Line Sub.	Game 2. Line Sub.	Game 3. Line Sub.	Game 4. Line Sub.	Game 5. Line Sub.

Court Positions	Game 1. Line Sub.	Game 2. Line Sub.	Game 3. Line Sub.	Game 4. Line Sub.	Game 5. Line Sub.
(1) Back R.					
(2) Front R.					
(3) Front C.					
(4) Front L.					
(5) Back L.					
(6) Back C.					

Name of Captain:
Name of Coach :

SCORES

Game 1.	1	2	3	4	5	6	7	8	9	10	11	12	13	14	15	16	17	18	19	20	21	22	Time - outs	Final score
TEAM (A)																								
TEAM (B)																								

Game 2.	1	2	3	4	5	6	7	8	9	10	11	12	13	14	15	16	17	18	19	20	21	22	Time - outs	Final score
TEAM (A)																								
TEAM (B)																								

Game 3.	1	2	3	4	5	6	7	⑧	9	10	11	12	13	14	15	16	17	18	19	20	21	22	Time - outs	Final score
TEAM (A)																								
TEAM (B)																								

FINAL SCORE OF THE MATCH:
: in favour of

Referee: Umpire: Scorer:

Official Volleyball Score Sheet of the Canadian Volleyball Association.

4. The referee holds something, such as a coin or rubber band, in the hand on the side nearest the serving team.

A valuable technique for the referee to follow is to keep one hand on the cable of the net while the ball is being served. This allows him to detect the slight touching of the net by a served ball.

It is also essential that prior to a match the referee:

1. Calls the two captains together and flips a coin to determine which team shall serve first and the teams' court positions. He also gives any final instructions on ground rules and informs them that should any question arise, only the captain should talk to the official involved.
2. Measures the height of the net at the center of the court.
3. Checks to see that there are no obstructions on or around the court and that spectators and substitute players are not seated in a hazardous location.

MINOR OFFICIALS

Since the referee is responsible for the conduct of the match, it is his duty to be sure that the minor officials (umpire, scorer, timekeeper, and linesmen) are aware of their duties and responsibilities prior to the match. It should also be understood that, if in the opinion of the referee a minor official makes a wrong decision, he has the power to overrule the decision. Although the referee has this authority, this does not minimize the importance of securing competent minor officials, since the success of any match depends very greatly upon their abilities. Many problems arise because of incompetent umpires, scorers, timekeepers, and linesmen.

The referee should instruct his officials as follows:

Umpire

1. Take position on side of court opposite the referee.
2. Make decisions regarding crossing of center line.
3. Assist in calling violations involving unsportsmanlike conduct and player out of position; authorize substitution; stop play for serious injury, or if a foreign object enters the court; and assist in any other way requested by the referee.
4. Be ready to accept time-out and substitution requests from playing captain, coach, or manager.
5. Keep official time of times-out, time allowed for injuries, and time between games.
6. Assist the scorer in verifying that the players are in their proper serving order prior to the start of the game.
7. It is the accepted practice that, at the time of the serve, the umpire observe the receiving team and the referee observe the serving team. However, the referee should instruct the umpire of his wishes.

Scorer*

1. Be seated on the side of the court opposite the referee.

2. Be responsible for the official scoring devices and records and record points as determined by the referee.

3. Secure names and numbers of starting players and their serving order. He shall verify that the players are in their proper serving order prior to the start of the game.

4. Notify the umpire when a player is in an incorrect position as soon after the serve as possible.

5. Keep official record of each team's times-out.

6. Record substitutions as reported.

7. Notify the referee during the third game of a match when a team scores eight points or after four minutes of ball in play, whichever comes first, for automatic change of court.

Timekeeper

1. Be seated beside scorer.

2. Start the clock the instant the server serves the ball and stop the clock the instant the ball is grounded or an official blows his whistle.

3. If no visible device is available to indicate the time remaining to play, he should call out the following numbers of minutes left to play when the ball is dead: four, two, and one.

Linesman

1. Notify the referee when the server touches a line bounding the service area or the floor outside this area at the instant the ball is hit by the server.

2. Indicate by using the official hand signals that the ball was "in" or "out" of court. These correspond to the "safe" and "out" signals used by baseball umpires.

3. Notify the referee if the serve or any played ball crossed the net outside the markers on the sides of the net.

4. During time-out, the linesman nearest the server shall hold the game ball. He shall give the ball to the server when the referee directs play to resume.

5. A ball touching any part of the boundary line is good.

---

* The USVBA has a national Committee on Official Scorers and Certification and publishes a *Volleyball Scorebook*. The official volleyball score sheet of the Canadian Volleyball Association is reproduced in this chapter as an example of an efficient scoring device. It may be ordered from CVA Publications, 78 Tedford Drive, Scarborough 4, Ontario, Canada.

6. Stand in the position designated by the referee. See the frontispiece for a diagram of the court.

7. Each linesman should have a whistle for notification purposes as called for in numbers 1 and 3 above.

Officiating volleyball is a team effort. If all officials are alert and perform their duties as prescribed, the playing teams will usually be satisfied. It is most important that the referee thoroughly instruct the umpire concerning his expectations. Some referees expect the umpire to call only violations including center line, unsportsmanlike conduct, player out of position, and injuries, while others expect him to call all plays if the player's back is to the referee. Still others ask the umpire to call all ball-handling violations whenever they are observed. Therefore, it is imperative that prior to the game the referee give complete instructions to his umpire as to his wishes.

It is considered good procedure for every official to attend one officials' clinic each year. No matter how competent an official may be, he needs practice after a layoff. Also, there are apt to be changes and new interpretations in the rules each year.

Let us again realize that volleyball is a game for the players. Officials should officiate the game according to the rules and not the way they, as individuals, would like to see the game played. They must insist on clean ball handling but not be so strict that volleyball becomes a whistle-tooting game lacking in player and spectator appeal. "Good officiating makes for enjoyable, uncontroversial games."[8]

There are two classifications of USVBA officials—Regional and National. It is necessary to be a Regional Official for one year before requesting to qualify as a National Official. To certify as a Regional Official, one should:

1. Make application to Regional Officials' Chairman.

2. Attend and participate in at least one recognized officials' clinic.

3. Demonstrate ability to officiate satisfactorily two matches under game conditions.

4. Pass written examination on USVBA rules.

5. Regional Officials must be recertified every third year.

Those who have attained and maintained the Regional Official status for one year or more and wish to certify as a National Official should:

1. Make direct application to the National Chairman of Officials and Certification Committee or contact their Regional Officials' Chairman to secure application. This application is then forwarded to the National Chairman of Officials and Certification Committee.

2. Demonstrate ability to officiate satisfactorily two matches under game conditions. The degree of proficiency must be higher than that for the Regional test.

3. Pass written examination on USVBA rules.
4. National Officials must recertify every fourth year.

Persons wishing to certify as either Regional or National Officials must wear the USVBA official's uniform at the time they demonstrate their ability to officiate. Upon certification, officials are expected to wear the uniform while officiating tournament matches. The official uniform is:

For Men:
  Shirt—A white tennis-type shirt having short sleeves and a collar and two or three buttons. The Regional or National Officials emblem over left breast.
  Pants—Black dacron and wool slacks.
  Shoes—White tennis shoes.
  Belt—Black.
  Jacket—Optional.

For Women:
  Shirt—Same as for men.
  Slacks—Black Koratron or dacron and wool.
  Shoes—White tennis shoes with white socks.
  Belt—Black, if needed.
  Jacket—Optional.

Shirts and jackets are custom made and can be ordered only from the National Officials' Chairman.

SAMPLE VOLLEYBALL CLINICS FOR OFFICIALS, COACHES, AND PLAYERS

Most of the clinics in the United States designed to improve the level of volleyball officiating have been one-day events. Some have been of shorter duration conducted in conjunction with a one-day tournament. A sample type of short clinic is outlined below, but more emphasis needs to be placed on longer clinics. Three-day clinics, as sponsored by the U. S. Army and U. S. Air Force at their overseas posts, are much more desirable and beneficial.

Sample #1—For one-day clinic
  9:00 a.m.   History of the game.
  9:15 a.m.   Rules of the game and their interpretation.
  10:00 a.m. Developing competence as a volleyball official.
      1. Procedure in becoming an official.
      2. Problems of the official.
      3. Marks of a good official.
      4. Minor officials and their responsibilities.
      5. Methods of calling and game control.
      6. Use of hand signals.

11:00 a.m.	Techniques of coaching and playing volleyball.

        1. The serve.
        2. The overhand pass.
        3. The set.
        4. The kill or spike.

12:00 noon Lunch

12:30 p.m. Volleyball Movie*

1:00 p.m. Continue techniques of coaching and playing volleyball.

        5. The block.
        6. Floor positions and floor coverage.
        7. The bump pass and variations.
        8. Warm-up drills.

3:00 p.m. Team games. Those wishing to certify as officials to be rated on their officiating ability.

4:30 p.m. Rules examination for officials.

5:00 p.m. Conclusion of clinic.

5:30 p.m. Presentation of officials' emblems to those who qualify. If time does not permit, they are notified by mail.

Sample #2—For three-day clinic

First Day

8:00 - 8:30 a.m. Registration.

8:30 - 9:20 a.m. Introduction of Clinic Instructors.
                     Plan for Clinic Presentations.
                     Lecture: "The Status of Volleyball as a Competitive Sport."

        A. History of Volleyball.
        B. Organizations promoting Volleyball.
        C. Reference materials.

9:30 -10:20 a.m. Techniques of Serving and Overhand Passing.

10:30 -11:20 a.m. Techniques of Bump Passing and Variations; Tests for Serving and Passing.

11:30 a.m.- 1:00 p.m. Lunch.

1:00 - 1:50 p.m. Volleyball Movie; Techniques of Setting.

2:00 - 2:30 p.m. Techniques of Spiking; Lecture on Rules.

3:00 - 3:50 p.m. Scrimmage between Teams.

Second Day

8:00 - 8:30 a.m. Lecture on Rules.

8:30 - 9:20 a.m. Techniques of Spiking and Blocking; Review of Serving and Passing Drills.

9:30 -10:20 a.m. Offensive and Defensive Formations: receiving the serve, 4-2 offense, 5-1 offense, 6-0 offense, shifting blockers, multiple blocks, back-court defense.

---

* See list of films in Selected Bibliography.

10:30	-11:20 a.m.	Scrimmage between Teams.
11:30 a.m.-	1:00 p.m.	Lunch.
1:00	- 1:50 p.m.	Volleyball Movie; Demonstration of Officiating Techniques.
2:00	- 2:50 p.m.	Review of Spiking and Blocking Drills.
3:00	- 3:50 p.m.	Scrimmage between Teams; Individuals practice Officiating.

Third Day

8:00	- 8:30 a.m.	Lecture on Rules.
8:30	- 9:20 a.m.	Officiating Techniques—Referee, Umpire, Linesmen, Timer, Scorer.
9:30	-10:20 a.m.	Scrimmage between Teams and Prospective Referees Officiate for Rating.
10:30	-11:20 a.m.	Same as above.
11:30 a.m.-	1:00 p.m.	Lunch.
1:00	- 1:50 p.m.	Review of Rules and Officiating Techniques.
2:00	- 2:50 p.m.	Scrimmage between Teams and Prospective Referees Officiate for Rating.
3:00	- 3:50 p.m.	USVBA Written Exam for Certification as Regional Volleyball Officials.

Those passing the final exam will be issued officials' cards and will be listed in *Official Volleyball Guide.*

INTERNATIONAL VARIATIONS*

Up until the 1967-68 volleyball season, there were substantial differences between officiating practices of USVBA officials and those of the International Volleyball Federation (FIVB). This condition was due mainly to the actual differences in rules. Since USVBA Rules have moved closer to International Rules, and International Rules have actually incorporated some principles basic to USVBA Rules, the variations in officiating should decrease during the coming years.

There still remain some obvious and subtle differences which are worthy of study. In the international game, one is impressed by the more formal nature of officiating. The referee is referred to as First Arbiter; the umpire, as Second Arbiter. The rights of the two arbiters are not equal. This is also true in the case of the Referee and Umpire of the USVBA, but, once again, the more formal approach to the matter is revealed in international competition. At the 1967 Pan American Games Volleyball Championships, Vladimir Savvin instructed all officials, "First referee is *first* referee."[9] Savvin, vice president of FIVB, came over from Moscow to be chairman of officials at this international championship.

Another example concerns the Linesmen. They are equipped with small

* This section is by J. Edmund Welch.

red flags. When a ball is out, the Linesman raises his flag instead of giving a simple hand signal. When the ball is in, the Linesman points his flag to the floor. This system is much clearer than the use of hand signals.

Still another example is the practice which requires the captain of each team to wear special insignia on his uniform. This stresses the rule that only the captain may address the First or Second Arbiter.

An international tournament has a jury to settle all disputes and to counsel coaches and officials. The jury watches all matches. It has separate meetings with coaches and with officials as the tournament progresses. In regard to officials, the jury advises each official during the tournament and tells him what he is doing right and what he is doing wrong. This body, though diplomatic, will not hesitate to correct an official in an officials' meeting. The jury, in its functioning, is more powerful than the USVBA Committee on Officials.

Another more formal approach concerns the coaches and players. Coaches may not enter the court during a time-out or time between games. Neither may the players leave the court, except during the special five-minute rest period between the fourth and fifth games.

In actual officiating technique, it is necessary for the First Arbiter to keep his hand on the net cable at all times during play in order to detect net touches. International players are not expected to call net touches or touches of the ball when an official has missed the play. Both the First Arbiter and the Second Arbiter must be especially alert to catch these plays. Those of us in the USVBA believe strongly that our system of having the players assist the officials by calling net touches and touches of the ball is much to be preferred. It fosters player integrity and a sense of trust between the officials and the players.

Rules interpretations by International officials have posed a big problem, not only for the USVBA, but for various national federations within FIVB. One rules interpretation has to do with the soft spike, sometimes referred to as a dink shot or dump spike. Primarily, this is a change of pace from the power smash, and the spiker often uses his fingers on the ball to make his placement over or to the sides of the block. Ten years ago this shot was almost always called a thrown ball by USVBA officials. The shot has been an important part of international strategy. A knowledgeable observer today will conclude that top spikers are very skillful with the soft spike and do not throw it except in a small percentage of the cases.

The second rules interpretation in international play continues to be a most important center of controversy. Certain leading referees of FIVB ruled prior to and during the 1964 Olympic Games that the overhand or chest pass in service receptions was a foul most of the time. This caused national teams from all over the world to resort to bumping the first pass to the front line by playing the ball off the forearms. The bumping technique replaced the overhand pass as the standard method of playing the first pass.

In September, 1966, the International Volleyball Federation issued a directive stating that the overhand pass in service receptions *can* be played in a legal manner. Officials' organizations throughout the world were advised to get away from hard rulings on service receptions. In November, 1966, the United States Volleyball Association followed up with a similar statement of officiating policy. The USVBA statement is worthy of direct quotation, "This is to inform you (USVBA officials) that it is not illegal to use a face or chest pass, as long as it is otherwise a legal play, and that any official who insists on applying rules that do not exist could be in danger of losing his Regional or National Rating."[10] At the 1967 Pan American Games, Vladimir Savvin instructed the officials to follow the directive of FIVB on this matter.[11]

Directives of FIVB and USVBA should be adhered to strictly by officials. Only in this way can the intent of the rules be properly interpreted for the benefit of the sport.

Both International and USVBA methods of officiating have certain special advantages and disadvantages. In the coming years, let us work to emphasize the advantages of both systems so that the goals for the sport of volleyball can be more readily attained.

REFERENCES

1. Nelson, Richard C., "Follow-up Investigation of the Velocity of the Volleyball Spike," *Research Quarterly*, March, 1964, p. 84.
2. Wardale, Peter, *Volleyball: Skills and Tactics* (London: Faber and Faber Limited, 1964), p. 113.
3. Walters, Marshall L., ed., *1969 Official Volleyball Guide* (Berne, Indiana: USVBA Printer), p. 181.
4. *Ibid.*, pp. 203-204.
5. Wardale, *op. cit.*, p. 120.
6. Odeneal, William T., "Basics of Officiating," *1966 Official Volleyball Guide* (Berne, Indiana: USVBA Printer), p. 115.
7. Wardale, *op. cit.*, p. 120.
8. *Ibid.*, p. 125.
9. Meeting of International Volleyball Officials, Winnipeg, Canada, July 23, 1967.
10. Official Directive from C. L. Bobb Miller, USVBA National Chairman of Officials, November 22, 1966.
11. Meetings of International Volleyball Officials, Winnipeg, Canada, July 23 and July 25, 1967.

See also the following references:

A. Appendix B in this book. This is the official directive of the International Volleyball Federation which declared that the overhand pass is legal in serve receptions.
B. Meltzer, Peter S., "Let's Take A Look At Officials," *1968 Official Volleyball Guide* (Berne, Indiana: USVBA Printer), pp. 121-124.
C. Carroll, Irwin J., "Reflections on Officiating Volleyball," *1962 Official Volleyball Guide* (Berne, Indiana: USVBA Printer), pp. 32-34.

9. Teaching Techniques

By RICHARD C. NELSON

IN the preceding chapters the fundamentals of volleyball have been discussed in detail. An instructor must have a thorough knowledge of the fundamentals of any sport before he can do a really good job of teaching. Methods and techniques of teaching are not sufficient without this grounding in the basic aspects of a sport. It is also true that a knowledge of the fundamentals alone is insufficient for the teacher or coach. He must know sound methods and techniques of imparting his knowledge to the student or player.

In this chapter the emphasis will be placed on the methods and techniques of teaching volleyball. This includes suggestions for teaching as well as appropriate drills and tests. Since there are probably as many unique teaching situations as there are teachers, a general approach to teaching has been followed. The material has been arranged in a logical manner progressing from the basic to the advanced levels. Certainly no instructor would have reason to use all the material presented. However, certain portions of it would be useful to all instructors, regardless of their teaching circumstances.

CLASS ORGANIZATION

During the first meeting the usual administrative matters dealing with the class must be covered. In addition, the introduction to the course may be given. This should include a general description of the game and a brief discussion of its history. If a short film covering this material is available, it could be shown at this time.

Before beginning the instruction phase, the class should be arranged in squads or teams. Reasonably balanced teams can be obtained by taking every fifth name (in the case of five teams) from the class roll. The number in each squad is usually dependent upon the class size and the number

143

of courts available. If possible, squads of six or seven students should be selected. If seven are selected, the additional man will cover absences and can rotate in smoothly during team play. For a coeducational class, a good ratio is two boys to one girl. The teams can then be composed of two girls as setters and four boys as spikers. Instructors who plan to have students officiate should divide the class into an odd number of teams. Thus, when a team is not scheduled to play, its members are called upon to officiate. The team rosters should be posted so the students can learn quickly their team number and the names of their teammates. A short warm-up should be conducted prior to each class period. Warm-up exercises should include push-ups on the fingertips, jumping, and sit-ups.

For maximum skill development there should be one ball for every two students. Since this situation seldom exists, well-organized group drills are essential for optimal learning. All available balls, including old and worn ones, should be used to keep the ratio of students per ball as low as possible. To motivate the students during the drills, competition between squads should be held whenever possible.

INDIVIDUAL FUNDAMENTALS AND DRILLS

The pass is usually introduced first. In order to avoid two mistakes which are common among students learning the mechanics of the pass, the instructor should emphasize: (1) the importance of moving under the ball, and (2) a high pass. The following are drills for developing passing skill. Those best suited for unskilled students are presented first.

Key to Diagrams
O—Setter or Passer; X—Spiker; $\overset{Y}{O}$—Blocker; ⟶ Path of Player;
– – –→ Path of Ball

Figure #26 shows the "pepper" drill. The leader passes alternately to the others as they return the pass to him. Each of the squad members is given an opportunity to act as the leader. The teacher can move from group to group and assume the leader's position. By so doing, he can both instruct and motivate the students and demonstrate the proper technique at the same time.

The circle passing drill[1] (Figure #27) involves passing the ball around a circle approximately twelve feet in diameter. If the squad has an even number of players, each pass goes to the next man in the circle. If the number is odd, the pass goes to the second player to the right of the passer. This drill stresses positioning the body so as to face the man to whom the pass is intended. A variation of this drill is to place one player in the center who passes alternately to the others as in the "pepper" drill.

The parallel line passing drill[2] (Figure #28) is especially useful in large classes when a limited number of balls are available. The two lines

Fig. 26. "Pepper" passing drill.

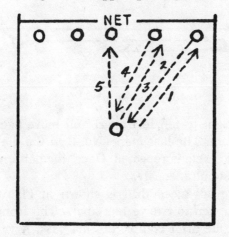

Fig. 27. Circle passing drills.

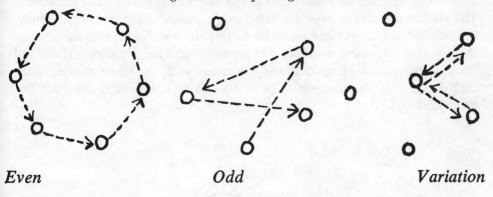

Even   *Odd*   *Variation*

Fig. 28. Parallel line passing drill.

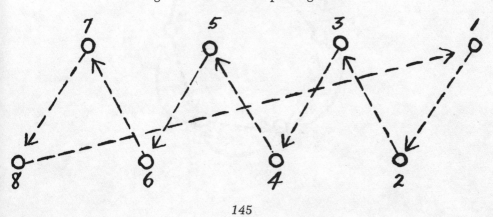

Fig. 29. File passing drill.

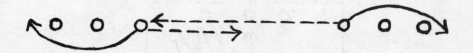

should start about eight to ten feet apart and move back as the students improve in ball control. The last man (No. 8 in the diagram) passes the ball to No. 1, and the cycle is repeated. Once this pattern is mastered, two balls may be passed simultaneously.

A somewhat more advanced drill is shown in Figure #29.[3] The two files are placed about ten to twelve feet apart. The front player moves to the rear of his own file after completing his pass. A variation is to have the passer move across (keeping to the right) to the end of the other file after completing his pass.[4]

The basket-pass drill, used where a basketball basket is available, is very popular among volleyball students. The squad forms a semicircle with a ten-foot radius about a point directly below the basket. The leader of the drill stands beneath the basket and passes alternately to the other members. The players attempt to pass the ball into the basket. Individual points may be awarded as follows: one point for hitting the backboard; two for hitting the rim, but not going through; and three for making a basket. These individual points can be totaled and compared with the other groups. This drill encourages the students to pass the ball high, which is essential for good passing.

Fig. 30. Passing drill.

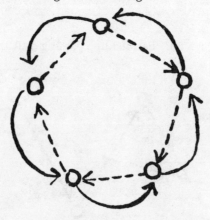

For advanced players the drill in Figure #30 may be used. The players jog in a counterclockwise direction while passing to the man in front. This is an excellent pregame warm-up drill.

The next fundamental introduced is the underhand bump or dig pass. The writer suggests teaching the double forearm technique first, later the single forearm technique. Emphasis should be placed on bumping or digging the ball up high enough so that a teammate can make the next pass. It should be mentioned again that bump and dig passes should be used only when a student is unable to make the overhand pass. Having taught this method, the instructor should insist upon its use in all underhand plays whether in drills or in scrimmage. The overhand pass drills in Figures #26, #27, and #29 can also be used for bump and dig passes.

Fig. 31. Dig pass drill for retrieving net balls.

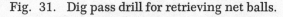
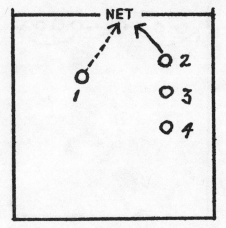

An excellent application of this pass is for use in retrieving the ball from the net. In figure #31, Player 1 tosses the ball into the net and says, "set" or "over." Player 2 on the command "set" attempts to dig the ball up to be spiked; if the command "over" is given, he tries to dig the ball up and over the net.

The next fundamental covered is the serve. The underhand serve should be introduced first, but those students who have the necessary strength and coordination should be taught the overhand floater serve as soon as possible.

An excellent beginning drill is to have the student serve against a wall from about fifteen feet away. To encourage accuracy, a target or line may be marked on the wall. Another drill may be used with one squad arranged along the end line of each court. One player is stationed on the court to receive the serves from the other side. He tosses the ball to the first player in his line, who then serves from the service area. After the serve, the retriever goes to the end of his line and is replaced by the player who just served. An advanced variation called "spot serving" can be employed as the students become proficient. The servers try to serve directly to the retriever on the other side of the net. The persons retrieving should move to different areas of the court. Another way to stress accurate placement of the serve is to chalk rectangular or circular targets on the courts, or use chairs as targets.

Once the serve has been introduced, the students should be given an opportunity to play during the last portion of the period. A minimum number

Fig. 32. Set drill.

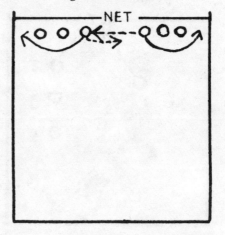

of rules should be given as they begin playing. The class periods can follow the pattern of reviewing drills of previous skills, introducing and drilling of the next fundamental, and finishing with loosely organized games. As more fundamentals are covered, refinement of the rules may be added.

The next fundamental in the progression is the set. This is usually difficult for the students to master. The two mistakes most frequently observed are: (1) failing to move the body into the proper position, and (2) not arching the ball high enough.

The file drill in Figure #29 can be used effectively for setting practice. The two files spaced fifteen feet apart should be parallel to the net as shown in Figure #32. After making the set, the student returns to the end of his line. This drill provides the players the opportunity of becoming properly oriented to the net during the set. This is essential before progressing to the more difficult drills.

Figure #33 shows an effective drill for developing this fundamental. No. 1 tosses to No. 4, who sets the ball for the retriever. He catches it and tosses to No. 2, who has assumed No. 1's position. After making their pass, the players move to the end of the opposite line. With more skillful players, the ball can be passed rather than tossed at each station.

A more advanced drill is performed by groups of three players.[5] They should start about four feet from the net. No. 1 stands at the left side line, No. 2 at the center, and No. 3 at the right side line. No. 1 passes to No. 2, who has a choice of returning to No. 1 or setting over his head to No. 3. No. 3 then either passes to No. 1 or No. 2 and the passing continues. They

Fig. 33. Set drill.

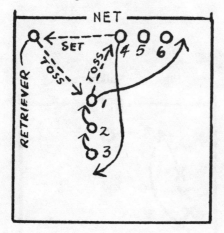

should change positions frequently. In large classes, a line on the floor may be used in place of the net.

Spiking, the most difficult of the basic skills, immediately follows the set. A majority of the time devoted to teaching the spike should be spent on the two-foot take-off technique. Since this skill is very complex, a suggested beginning is to have the students first execute the approach and jump without a ball.

Wall spiking[6] is one of the most widely used methods of developing this skill. The student starts by driving the ball to the floor close to the wall. The ball will bounce up to the wall and rebound out to the spiker, who jumps up again and spikes it to the floor. This drill gives the instructor a good chance to observe whether the student is imparting overspin to the ball. A soft ball permits the player to hit the ball hard on each play. Handball courts are very useful for wall spiking. A game with two players hitting the ball alternately can easily be developed.

The next step is to lower the nets one and one-half feet below the normal height and employ the drill in Figure #34. The first player in the spiking line should be about eight to ten feet from the net. He then approaches the net and spikes the ball which has been tossed up by the setter. This provides for a high percentage of good sets, which makes the drill run more smoothly. The players return to the end of the line after spiking. The job of tossing the ball up should be rotated among the team members. Spiking should be practiced from both the left and right sides. Gradually the nets should be raised as skill improves until they are back to their normal height.

Blocking, the main defensive maneuver against the spike, can be combined with the spiking drills. Individual blocking fundamentals may be practiced by having the players line up facing the net and jump to block an imaginary ball.

Fig. 34. Spiking drill.

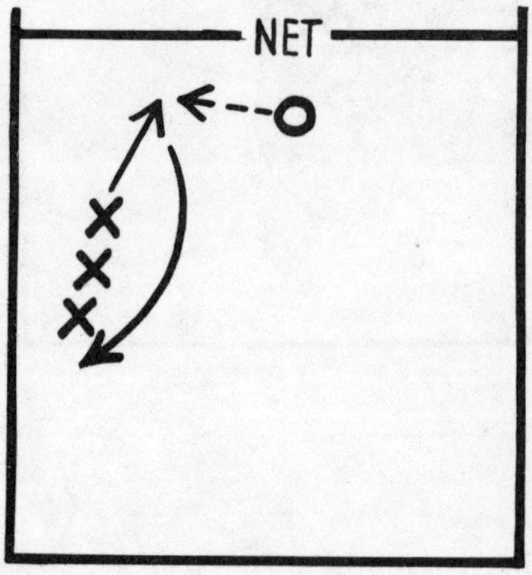

All of the previous drills have been limited to the one fundamental being taught. Since volleyball requires such a high degree of team play, it is important that students understand and practice this phase of the game. For this reason, the following combination drills are presented.

The first of these combines the set and spike. In Figure #35, No. 2 tosses the ball to No. 1, who in turn sets for No. 3. A modification of this

Fig. 35. Set-spike drill.

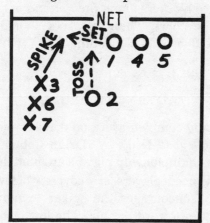

drill[7] would be to use another line of spikers on the right side. With a spiker on each side, the setter then has the option of setting forward or back over his head. A further addition to these variations would be to have a player toss the ball to No. 2 from across the net. Instead of tossing the ball to No. 1, No. 2 passes to him.

Figure #36 shows the addition of blocking to the previous drill. One and two-man blocks can be practiced during this drill. If desired, spiking and blocking can be done from only one side at a time. The spikers and

Fig. 36. Set-spike-block drill.

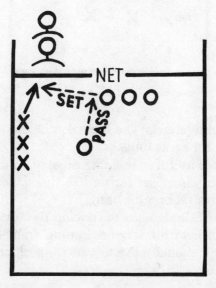

blockers exchange positions after every five plays. A more advanced version would be to place three blockers along the net and a spiker on both the left and right sides of the court. These blockers should attempt to form a two-man block on either side depending upon which player does the spiking.

ADVANCED DRILLS

The most modern and complete work on drills for advanced players may be found in *Power Volleyball Drills* by Harlan Cohen.[8] Fifty-eight drills or procedures to develop championship players are included.

Four drills for advanced players are covered below. The first of these shown in Figure #37 encourages the spiker to move quickly—laterally first and then straight in toward the net. The low or quick set can be used

Fig. 37. Advanced spike drill.

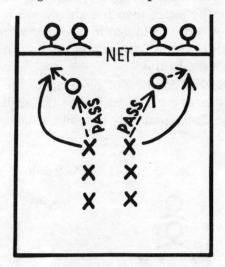

to develop a fast-hitting attack. The inclusion of the blockers provides for defensive practice at the same time.

A variation of this is useful in building deception into the attack (Figure #38). The setter can either set forward to the spiker on the left or give the other spiker a quick set over his head.

The drill in Figure #39 is used to develop the "first set" attack. It also helps the spikers learn to hit sets originating from the back court. The player setting the ball should move to various positions in the center and back areas of the court.

Fig. 38. Spiking drill—optional set.

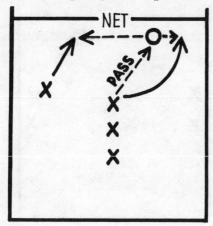

The present-day international style of play includes the use of a back-line player as the setter. By so doing, any one of the three front-line players is free to spike. Figure #40 displays a drill to develop this style of attack. The setter can set wide to either outside spiker or low to the center forward.

If enough courts are available, teams of less than the regulation six

Fig. 39. "First set" spiking drill.

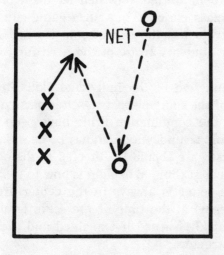

Fig. 40. Three spiker attack drill.

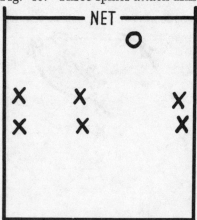

players may be organized. Examples are two-man teams or doubles, three-man teams, and four-man teams. Mixed doubles can be played also.

The advantage in reducing the number of players lies in developing the ability to move quickly on the court. Defensively, the block is minimized and emphasis placed on back-line digs of the spiked balls. The popularity of doubles play in California is a primary reason for the many fine defensive players there.

DISCUSSION

During the instruction of individual fundamentals, the students will become extremely anxious to scrimmage. The teacher can explain only enough rules to get them started and then let them play during the last few minutes of the class period. Thus, in a game situation, they will be given the opportunity to use the skills being learned in the drills. This should also make the students aware of the need for further work on the fundamentals.

Following the completion of the individual skills, team fundamentals are introduced. Use of the four-spiker, two-setter pattern of team organization is preferred. If the combination drills have been used, the general offensive pattern should be understood. It may be necessary to re-emphasize the point that the first pass should be directed to the center forward who acts as the setter. The first thing to explain is how to switch positions along the front line so the setter is always in the center after the serve. The alignment of both teams at the time of the serve is also covered. These patterns are more quickly learned if explained and then diagramed on a blackboard by the instructor.

The students are now ready to receive instruction in officiating. The duties of the referee, umpire, and linesmen should be explained fully. The instructor can illustrate by refereeing a short match between two of the teams. Emphasis should be placed on calling carries or held balls. It is only through reasonably strict officiating that improvement in ball handling can be obtained. This introduction to officiating should be accompanied by a more detailed explanation of the rules. These rules should be condensed on one mimeographed sheet and distributed to the students.

Most high school and college students have never witnessed two good teams in action. As a result, they seldom realize that volleyball involves more than merely batting the ball over the net. It is important, therefore, to expose them to competitive volleyball if possible. This may be done through a game film or a demonstration by skilled players if either is available. It is probably most effective to do this when team fundamentals are being practiced.

The remainder of the class lessons is spent primarily on team play. After team fundamentals have been practiced, the writer suggests using two periods for a round robin of short ten-minute practice games with the students also being exposed to the job of officiating. By noting the scores, a comparison of the teams can be made. If considerable differences exist, a change of one or two key players is usually enough to bring the teams to the same approximate level. When this phase has been completed, the teams follow a full round-robin schedule, playing one match per day. During these periods the instructor has an opportunity to obtain a subjective rating of each student's playing and officiating ability. The instructor should note the mistakes being made by individuals or teams as a whole and correct them at the end of the period.

Since the class time is usually limited, the games may be played to eleven instead of fifteen points. In this way more games are completed and a better comparison of the teams can be obtained. The wins and losses should be recorded and posted daily. One of the most common early mistakes observed in team play is an overanxiety to get the ball over the net. In many cases the play becomes similar to a ping-pong game with only one hit being used by each team. This can be easily discouraged by making an addition to the rules as follows. If a player returns the ball over the net on the first pass, his team loses the volley as if they had hit it out of bounds. Exceptions would be made when blocking the ball at the net, digging a hard-driven spike, and spiking an opponent's return near the net. This rule forces the players to think in terms of directing the first pass to the setter.

Some additional suggestions to improve the course should be mentioned. Oftentimes the nets are not sufficiently taut to allow the players to retrieve the ball out of them. This can be overcome by taping a three-foot broom handle or hockey stick to the ends of the net. This spreads the net out evenly and these end pieces can then be fastened tightly to the standards with heavy string or rope. To further improve the net, a piece of clothes-line rope should be taped along the bottom of the net. This helps the net flip the ball back into play rather than allowing it to fall to the floor.

Another feature that makes the game move more smoothly is the use of scoreboards. These can be made from a two-foot by four-foot board by painting two clock surfaces numbered from zero to fifteen on them. A hand or dial on each clock is attached with a small spring which keeps the hand from slipping. The board can be placed just off the court and the player nearest the board can move the dial as points are scored. Thus, the players know the score at all times, and the usual confusion concerning the score is eliminated.

VOLLEYBALL TESTS

Tests in volleyball take two forms—the skill test and the written test. The skill test measures a student's or player's ability to perform certain aspects of the game such as serving or passing. Some of these tests have been correlated with general volleyball playing ability. The written test measures such factors as knowledge of rules, history of volleyball, and strategy.

Tests, depending on the type, can be important for grading, measuring teacher effectiveness, predicting the ability of players, classifying players into teams of equal strength, comparing the skill and progress of players, diagnosing individual weaknesses, and stimulating player interest. Some skill tests, such as serving tests, can be used effectively in the instructional phase of the program.

A volleyball test can be of maximum effectiveness if it meets the following requirements. First, is the test valid, does the test measure accurately what it intends to measure? For example, does a wall volley test actually measure general playing ability? Second, is the test reliable, does it measure consistently what it intends to measure? For example, if the wall volley test is given to a class on different occasions, will similar results be obtained?

The statistical concepts of validity and reliability give us a common denominator from which to judge and select tests. If Test A has higher validity and reliability coefficients than Test B, then we can safely assume that Test A is better.

Unfortunately, there are just a few volleyball tests which have been subjected to statistical analysis and meet acceptable standards for both validity and reliability. Since most of these tests were devised, there have been many changes in playing techniques, officiating, and rules. The validity of some of these tests could possibly be questioned now. However, the approach which the authors took was statistically sound. Their scientific method points the way toward developing new volleyball tests at the various levels of play.

Brady developed a wall volley test designed to measure the general volleyball playing ability for college men.[9] He found the test to be useful with college men as a classifying device, as one basis for grading, and as a measure of skill improvement. A horizontal chalk line is drawn on the wall five feet in length and eleven feet six inches from the floor. Then a vertical line is drawn upward from each end of the five-foot horizontal line to complete the target area. The student may choose to stand at any distance from the wall. He throws the ball against the wall and then volleys it against the specified area on the wall. If he makes an illegal volley or if the ball gets away from him, he starts again as in the beginning. His score is the number of successful volleys in one minute.

Three relatively recent studies concerning the skill of executing the overhand pass are reported in the *Research Quarterly*. Krongvist and Brumbach modified the Brady test for use with high school boys.[10] Clifton devised a single hit volley test for college women.[11] Whereas Krongvist and Brumbach designed their test to measure the overall volleyball playing ability of the students, Clifton's test measures only the specific skill of volleying. Likewise, Liba and Stauff devised a test for the one skill of executing the overhand pass.[12] Their test can be used with college women, and a slight modification of it is applicable with junior high school girls.

Mohr and Haverstick did a most significant study in 1956 which hit upon factors considered to be extremely vital today in the training of Pan American and Olympic volleyball players.[13] These two authors found that there was a relationship between jumping ability and volleying skill, and also between agility and volleying skill. This study emphasized the importance of teachers and coaches using agility exercises and jumping practice with their students and players. These training methods, or variations of them, are those which have made the difference in the great advance of United States national teams during the past five years.

A big problem in teaching volleyball to students is knowing which skills to introduce at each age level and what teaching techniques to employ. Many coaches feel that the future growth of volleyball as a competitive sport is linked closely to the correct instruction of students from the elementary school level right on through college. Whether one views volleyball as a coach or a teacher, studies involving such factors as achievement, jumping ability, agility, maturation, strength, and student ratings are very important and will become more important in the future.

Written tests take many forms, such as true-false, matching, multiple-choice, completion, and essay. Tests often take the form of a combination of some of the above. To construct a good written test is no easy task. A study of the techniques employed in sound test contruction should be beneficial to the volleyball instructor. These techniques are covered in many of the tests and measurements books in physical education and psychology.

Hooks constructed a written volleyball test for college students which met acceptable standards of validity and reliability.[14] This multiple-choice test has been revised to conform to the 1969 USVBA Rules and is included in Appendix C.

Testing should be a part of every instructional program. Many authorities believe that one-tenth of program time spent in testing is justifiable.[15]

CONCLUSION

Many suggestions and drills have been presented in this chapter as teaching aids for volleyball instructors and coaches. The suggestions and drills cover a variety of playing levels, but much of the material can be adapted to meet different situations.

As mentioned earlier, the instructor or coach needs a thorough knowledge of the fundamentals of volleyball in order to teach the game successfully. This chapter has stressed a second requirement for the successful teaching of volleyball—a mastery of sound teaching methods. Lastly, the successful teacher or coach needs diligence, patience, and enthusiasm.

REFERENCES

1. Emery, Curtis Ray, *Modern Volleyball* (New York: The Macmillan Company, 1953), p. 83.
2. Bush, Wayne L., "Volleyball Drills for the Gym Class and Varsity Squad," *Journal of Physical Education*, May-June, 1950, p. 104.
3. *Ibid.*
4. Emery, *op. cit.*, p. 83.
5. *Ibid.*, pp. 83-84.
6. *Ibid.*, p. 85.
7. Bush, *op. cit.*, p. 103.
8. Cohen, Harlan, *Power Volleyball Drills* (Hollywood, California: Creative Sports Books, P. O. Box 2244, 1966).
9. Brady, George F., "Preliminary Investigation of Volleyball Playing Ability," *Research Quarterly*, March, 1945, p. 14.
10. Krongvist, Roger A., and Brumbach, Wayne B., "A Modification of the Brady Volleyball Skill Test for High School Boys," *Research Quarterly*, March, 1968, p. 116.
11. Clifton, Marguerite A., "Single Hit Volley Test for Women's Volleyball," *Research Quarterly*, May, 1962, p. 208.
12. Liba, Marie R., and Stauff, Marilyn R., "A Test for the Volleyball Pass," *Research Quarterly*, March, 1963, p. 56.
13. Mohr, Dorothy R., and Haverstick, Martha J., "Relationship Between Height, Jumping Ability, and Agility to Volleyball Skill," *Research Quarterly*, March, 1956, p. 74.
14. Hooks, Edgar W., Jr., "Hooks' Comprehensive Knowledge Test in Selected Physical Education Activities for College Men," *Research Quarterly*, December, 1966, p. 506.
15. Clarke, H. Harrison, *Application of Measurement to Health and Physical Education* (fourth edition; Englewood Cliffs, N. J.: Prentice-Hall, 1967), p. 34.

See also the following references:

A. Cunningham, Phyllis, and Garrison, Joan, "High Wall Volley Test for Women's Volleyball," *Research Quarterly*, October, 1968, pp. 486-490.

B. Davis, Patricia A., "A Manual for Teaching Attack Volleyball to High School Students and Beginners" (unpublished M.Ed. thesis, University of North Carolina, Greensboro, North Carolina, 1966).

C. Doherty, John P., "Old Volleyballs Never Die," *The Physical Educator*, May, 1968, p. 87.

D. "Drills for Improvement of Basic Movement Requirements in Volleyball," *1966 Canadian Volleyball Annual and Rule Book*, CVA Publications, 78 Tedford Drive, Scarborough, Ontario, Canada, pp. 55-61.

E. Friermood, Harold T., ed., *Volleyball Skills Program*. Sponsored by U. S. Olympic Committee and U. S. Volleyball Association, 1966, revised 1967. Available from USVBA Commissioner of Regions, 13 State Street, Schenectady, New York. Also published in *1967 Official Volleyball Guide* (Berne, Indiana: USVBA Printer).

F. Geisler, Fred W., "Volleyball," *Journal of Health, Physical Education, Recreation*, January, 1966, pp. 31, 49.

G. Keiser, Helen E., "Volleyball Circuit Training," *The Physical Educator*, May, 1967, pp. 69-72.

H. Lowell, John C., "Volleyball Skill Test for College Men" (unpublished M.S. thesis, Brigham Young University, Provo, Utah, 1965).

I. McManama, Jerre, and Shondell, Don, "Teaching Volleyball Fundamentals," *Journal of Health, Physical Education, Recreation*, March, 1969, p. 43.

J. Singer, Robert N., "Sequential Skill Learning and Retention Effects in Volleyball," *Research Quarterly*, March, 1968, pp. 185-194.

K. Welch, J. Edmund, "First Volleyball Camp in the U.S.A.," *Journal of Physical Education*, September-October, 1968, pp. 18-19.

L. Wickstrom, R. L., "Modified Games for Practicing Volleyball," *The Physical Educator*, October, 1968, pp. 135-136.

10. A Game For Girls and Women

By MARY FRANCES KELLAM

IF actual count were taken, one would possibly find that more girls and women participate in the game of volleyball than do boys and men. It has long been a popular sport for women of all ages. Owing to the fact that girls can play with skills comparable to boys of the same age, it is an excellent co-educational activity. In most schools, elementary through colleges, the game is the number one sport in the physical education curriculum.

However, for years the game of volleyball for girls has actually been spoiled by poor teaching or no teaching. The ball has been thrown out onto the court, the court has been overcrowded, and the players have hit the ball back and forth with very little purpose in mind. It is easy to improve the skills and techniques of the players. Start them off correctly in the elementary school. Teach the proper techniques and modify the game only by lowering the net and altering the size of the court. Make the game a challenge and the results will soon be evident.

Teachers and coaches in our schools and colleges must become familiar with the modern skills and techniques of play. Plays that were once thought impossible for girls are now accepted. Rules are changing so that these skills are necessary to play the official game.

OFFICIAL RULES

At the present time there are two organizations governing volleyball play for girls and women, namely, the Division for Girls' and Women's Sports of the American Association for Health, Physical Education, and Recreation (DGWS) and the United States Volleyball Association (USVBA).

Both organizations formulate rules and publish separate volleyball guides. The USVBA's Rules for girls and women are the same as its rules for the boys and men, with the exception pertaining to the height of the net. The DGWS Rules are quite similar to those of the USVBA with a few exceptions. In addition to these two sets of rules, a third set is being employed—those of the International Volleyball Federation.

Although the games are basically alike, minor differences may make for some complications. Girls' and women's groups in the schools and colleges of the United States usually play according to DGWS rules. Outside the schools and colleges, girls and women, as well as boys and men, compete under USVBA Rules. All international competition, Olympic Games, and Pan American Games, as well as games played in foreign countries, use the International Rules. (USVBA Rules are now quite similar to International Rules.)

A great deal of work has been done in the United States to try to get one set of rules into operation. Through the years the USVBA and DGWS rules have come closer together. The concern now is really not the rules but the proper teaching of skills and techniques.

Because the individual techniques and system of play are so similar to those of the men's game, the chapters in this book that apply to individual techniques are applicable for teaching women and girls to play volleyball.

FUNDAMENTAL SKILLS

There are many fundamental skills required to play the game of volleyball effectively. Volleyball should be a fast game of skill, coordination, agility, and speed. It requires strength, anticipation, and ability to move quickly with fast reactions. However, the most important skill that must be learned, practiced, and understood is that of correct body position. Before a girl can successfully master the techniques and skills of the game, she must learn to move into and assume the correct body position. To play the ball properly using an overhand pass, single or double forearm pass, overhand serve, or a spike, the ball must be in front of the body and the body must face the direction of the intended ball flight. Once this is learned, the girl's skills will improve and she will play with a much greater degree of success.

A most successful way of teaching and practicing correct body position is by the use of a wall. This may be a gym wall, tennis backboard, handball court, or the outside of a school building. The wall allows the ball to be returned to the person exactly as it is hit. A player will soon learn that the ball must be in front of the body to hit it properly.

WALL DRILLS WITH THE OVERHAND PASS
FOR BODY POSITIONING[1]

1. Stand about four feet from the wall. Position one foot in front of the other and allow only the front foot to move. The ball must rebound at least six feet high on the wall, twenty-five to fifty times in succession.

2. Increase the distance from the wall to about six feet. At this distance, the ball should rebound at least eight feet in height for the same number of successive hits.

3. A more advanced drill to teach body positioning is the corner wall drill. The student passes the ball against one wall, then positions herself behind the ball with her feet and body now facing the wall to her right. She then contacts the ball with the body already turned and passes it against the corner wall which she is now facing. On the next pass, she must turn her body back to the left, facing the wall from which she originally started the drill. This will teach her to get her body behind the ball in order to control it. The ball must be hit at least fifteen feet in the air to give the student a chance to make the correct turn.

4. Divide the students into groups of four and form them into squares. The ball should be passed first in a clockwise and then in a counterclockwise direction. This offers the same drill for body positioning as the corner wall drill. For this drill to be effective, the girl receiving the pass must be behind the ball, facing in the direction of her intended pass. The ball must be passed high to give the students time to make the turn. It is important to teach the student that she does not face the person passing the ball to her but must move to the ball so that her side faces the person passing the ball. The ball must cross in front of her body before contact as she faces the direction of the pass.

THE OVERHAND PASS

There are several theories as to where the ball should contact the fingers. The finger tips are not recommended. The inside of the fingers, the fleshy part including possibly the first and second joints, will be most successful.

The ball should be received so that the player can see the ball and the back of her hands. This will put the actual play directly in front of the eyes. The fingers should be spread, the wrists should be flexed, and the ball should be played with stiff or tightened fingers. The legs are apart, the knees are slightly flexed, and one foot is forward.

If the ball is played as stated above, it will not hurt the fingers and it will not flip off the fingers in a backward direction. This also may keep a player from contacting the ball too high above the head.

There definitely has to be some strengthening of the hands and wrists for the girls to play the ball properly. Warm-ups with the girls hitting the ball back and forth against the wall with just the hands and wrists will be helpful.

DRILLS FOR STRENGTHENING HANDS AND WRISTS[2]

1. Stand about three or four feet away from the wall. Pass the ball rapidly against the wall using only wrist action. Contact the ball using the inside surface of the fingers. Do not emphasize height but emphasize rapid wrist action. Distance may be increased to six feet.
2. Stand three or four feet away from the wall. Using only wrist action, work on passing the ball to a height of eight feet or more. The distance may be marked on the wall with masking tape.
3. Stand six feet away from the wall. Hit the ball against the wall using the overhand serve. Receive the ball and attempt to pass it above a ten-foot line on the wall. Increase the power of the serve and also serve the ball lower on the wall. This will give practice in bending the knees in order to have the ball in front of the eyes. The forearm or bump pass may also be used to return this ball.

DOUBLE FOREARM PASS

This pass is most successful for the return of a hard-driven spike or a hard overhand serve and should always be used in place of a two-hand underhand pass.

There are several hand positions for the double forearm pass. An easily obtained and very effective arm position for girls is as follows: (1) place the back of one hand in the palm of the other; (2) straighten the arms; (3) rotate the elbows inward. The forearms should form a flat surface on which to bump the ball. The player should asume the proper body position, bend the knees, and place the arms low. The ball should contact the middle of the forearms. Wait for the ball to come to the forearms and as it hits, straighten the legs. The ball will then be bumped off the forearms.

In addition to strong hands and wrists, girls need strong legs and the ability to get quickly in position for low balls. Knee pads will not only protect the knees but will eliminate fear and, therefore, make it possible for a greater number of recoveries. A player should not hesitate to squat for low balls or even drop to one or both knees.

DRILLS FOR RECEIVING LOW BALLS[3]

1. Use a line abreast formation with a leader out in front. The leader throws the ball in a downward flight. The girl moves in position and returns the ball with an overhand pass or a double forearm pass.
2. Use the same formation as #1. The leader uses an overhand serve or spiking action. This makes a harder faster ball to return. Player moves into position and returns the ball as in #1.

3. Leader stands on a chair or stands on the opposite side of the net. The ball is thrown in a downward motion over the net. Players all face the net in the receiving-of-serve position. An overhand pass or a double forearm pass is used to send the ball to the center forward. To increase the speed of the ball, the leader may use an overhand serve or a spiking motion. Players should experience playing on the front and back line.

THE SPIKE

Girls must also be trained to jump. The spike cannot be successful without the ability to jump. As in other sports, getting the girls off the floor can be a difficult task. Drills and practice in the two-foot take-off should take place before the actual teaching of the spike. This practice should continue throughout the volleyball unit, emphasizing the need for developing greater height in each jump. Refer to the chapter on the spike for the suggested technique for performing the skill.

The following points need emphasis in teaching the girls. The take-off or approach will include more steps and the girl will possibly start from a more crouched position than the boys. This usually enables her to get more height. The take-off is taken as the ball is set, and both arms should be raised vigorously. Raising the nonhitting arm to maximum height is a "must." The hitting arm is raised in a bent position. The elbow leads and continues upward to approximately head height. The hand follows to this position and then the elbow is dropped downward, with the forearm and hand becoming perpendicular to the upper arm. As the arm comes down and the hand hits the ball, there is a flexing of the wrist and a whipping movement of the arm, wrist, and hand. The ball is hit with the heel of the hand or a cupped hand. Be sure the elbow leads in the upward action and the first downward movement. Avoid a straight arm, as this will result in a loss of power and in a tendency to throw the ball. The height of the ball for the spike will be determined by the individual and her ability to get up in the air.

DRILLS FOR TEACHING THE SPIKE[4]

1. Running in place on toes.
2. Jumping in place.
3. Sargent Jump.
4. Practice the action of the spike without the ball.
5. Practice hitting the ball out of the hand to the floor.
6. Have partner toss the ball in front of spiker. Keep ball about eight feet so that spiker is able to come down on it.

7. Same drill as #6 except the spiker jumps from standing position about ten feet. Spiker starts with side to net and ends facing the net.

8. Same drill as #7 except the spiker precedes the jump with steps or run.

The serve and the set are both handled in chapters in this book. The material is applicable to teaching girls.

Once the skills and techniques are acquired, put them into some pattern of play. Get away from the "pat-a-pat" game of volleyball. Just getting the ball back over the net has been the only concern of girls for too long. From the beginning, enforce the rules of throwing, holding, and pushing. Develop some basic patterns of play and make volleyball the team game that it is. Start with simple patterns that all can grasp, and use more difficult ones as the playing ability of the group is improved. As the teamwork improves, the game will become more fun. Each player should know her role in the total team effort.

DEFENSIVE PATTERNS OF PLAY

Receiving the Serve

When the opponents serve, the receiving team should place themselves into the strongest formation possible and one that can be easily changed to offense. Most of the serves will be placed to the center of the court or across it. This means the defensive formation should be in this area. Check the chapter in this book on defense for possible formations.

A basic pattern for receiving the serve and one used often by girls is as follows.

Fig. 41. Serve reception formation.

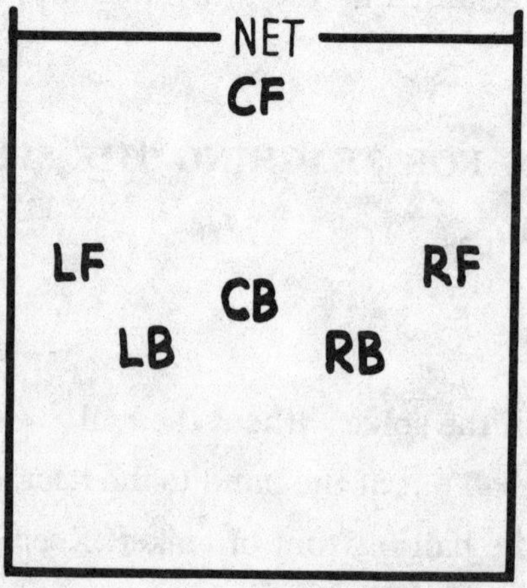

This formation provides five receivers, each with a specific area to cover and each with a clear view of the server. The sixth player is placed closer to the net and in a position to receive the pass and make a good set for the left forward or right forward. Players should be ready to back each other up and to recover any misplayed balls. All players should face the approaching ball and be ready to receive and pass.

The Block

The other defensive weapon is the block, which is the weakest part of most of the girls' games. A one, two, or three-player block may be used. The type of block used will depend upon the abilities of the players. For example, the three-player block would not be advisable when some of your players are short and unable to extend hands and arms above the net. You will find that most girls employ the two-player block. Much practice must be given to blocking in order for your players to develop the jump and the proper timing and to eliminate a fear of that hard-driven spike. There is a great feeling of satisfaction and accomplishment derived from blocking that spike.

In learning how to block, a person should practice jumping from standing position about two feet in front of the net. The jump should be from both feet, and the body is straight with the arms tilted forward. The blocker should jump at the same time of the spiker. The arms should be thrust upward and together. The fingers are spread and tilted slightly backward. When the spike is made, the fingers tense in readiness for the oncoming ball. The wrists of the blocker should be in line with and just above the net. When the blockers come down, they should look immediately for the ball.

OFFENSIVE PATTERNS OF PLAY

In receiving the ball, the players should be in a position of readiness to play the ball immediately with a pass, a set, and a spike or hit. No matter what offensive system of play you use, this 1-2-3 pattern of handling the ball is the most consistent.

Two highly recommended systems of play for girls and women are as follows:

Three-Three

This system should be used by beginners until the basic skills and techniques have really been mastered. This system has three set players and three hitters. The ball is always passed to a set player who sets it for one of her attack players.

Fig. 42. 3-3 offense with setter in CF position.

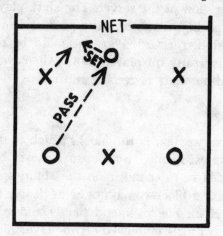

X — Spiker;   O — Setter;   ⟶ Path of player;   - - → Path of ball.

All players must move into position to cover the court and back up. Anticipating plays and getting in position is essential if good play is to result. Taller players will find it easier to spike and block, but, with the designated positions, the shorter player can discover the importance of being able to set the ball for the perfect spike. Without a good set, there can never be an effective spike.

Fig. 43. 3-3 Offense with setter in RF position.

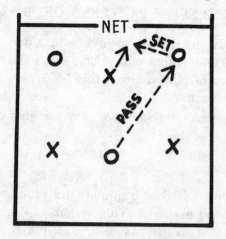

X — Spiker;   O — Setter;   ⟶ Path of player;   - - → Path of ball.

Four-Two

This system is a style of play that can be used with success by the more highly skilled women and girls. It can be used only when the playing rules allow the interchange of positions. USVBA Rules already do this, DGWS will be experimenting with this type of play, and in the very near future, this interchange should be a part of the rules. If the setter is not playing in the center forward position, she switches to this position after the ball is served. She always switches in front of and closer to the net than the spiker. The two setters carry the responsibility for guiding the team in the formation and the execution of plays.

In addition to individual skills a player must want to be a team player. She must accept each teammate as an equal and work constantly to help form six players into one skillful unit. This has to be instilled in the girls from the beginning. Once the girls get the fundamentals of play, they must work hard toward making this a team game.

OFFICIATING

In the United States, we are concerned mainly with USVBA officiating, which has been covered in Chapter 8, and DGWS officiating. Any women's team expecting to compete in USVBA state, regional, and national tournaments must be completely familiar with officiating practices of that ruling body. Women can become certified as both Regional and National Officials of the USVBA, and we have women serving in these capacities. Also, the USVBA has a plan to qualify Certified Scorers. The Official Score Sheet of the USVBA is a very detailed analysis of game play, and its use requires special training. Serving as Certified Scorers is another means by which men and women are contributing to the USVBA program.

For many years the Division for Girls' and Women's Sports has had a very well-organized plan to certify officials. Volleyball officiating is controlled by Affiliated Boards of Officials. Almost every state has at least one Affiliated Board, and a large state, such as California, may have as many as eleven of these boards. Although an Affiliated Board has the authority to rate officials in four categories, it in turn is responsible to national committees and an executive board of the Officiating Services Area. Detailed information on the DGWS plan may be found in the DGWS *Volleyball Guide*. Such matters as standards for officials ratings, volleyball study questions on rules, and lists of officiating boards and committees are all included.

The four ratings are The National Rating, The Local Rating, The Associate Rating, and The Intramural Rating. Special aids for DGWS officiating are as follows:

"Techniques of Volleyball Officiating," DGWS *Volleyball Guide*, 1965-1967, pp. 94-99.

Bell, Mary M., "Let's Be Official," DGWS *Volleyball Guide*, 1967-1969, pp. 61-62.

Harris, Dorothy V., "The Ideal Volleyball Official," DGWS *Volleyball Guide*, 1967-1969, pp. 63-65.

Barnes, Mildred J., *Program in Self-Instruction for Officiating DGWS Volleyball Rules* (Minneapolis, Minn.: Burgess Publishing Company, 1965).

Official Volleyball Scorebook, Division for Girls' and Women's Sports, AAHPER, 1201 Sixteenth Street, N.W., Washington, D.C. 1958.

REFERENCES

1. Ward, Jane, "Volleyball—A New Approach," DGWS *Volleyball Guide*, July, 1965-July, 1967, pp. 32-35. Published by AAHPER.
2. *Ibid.*
3. *Ibid.*
4. Laveaga, Robert E., *Volleyball* (New York: The Ronald Press Company, 1960), pp. 45-53.

See also the following references:

A. Jensen, Judith L., "The History and Development of Volleyball for Girls and Women" (unpublished M.S. thesis, Ohio State University, Columbus, Ohio, 1959).
B. Part III (Volleyball), *Proceedings, Fourth National Institute on Girls' Sports*, AAHPER, 1201 Sixteenth Street, N.W., Washington, D.C., 1968.
C. Series of articles in DGWS *Volleyball Guide*, July, 1965-July, 1967; DGWS *Volleyball Guide*, July, 1967-July, 1969. Available from AAHPER.

Selected Bibliography

BOOKS

Anthony, Don, *Volleyball: Do It This Way*. London: John Murray Company, 50 Albemarle Street, 1964. Available in the U.S. from Sportshelf, P. O. Box 634, New Rochelle, N.Y.

Boyden, E. Douglas, and Burton, Roger G., *Staging Successful Tournaments*, Second Edition. New York: Association Press, 1968.

Cherebetiu, Gabriel, *Fundamentos técnicos del Voleibol Moderno*. Mexico City: Comite Olimpico Mexicano, 1966.

_____, *Volleyball Techniques*. Hollywood, California: Creative Sports Books, P. O. Box 2244, 1968. (English translation of previous reference.)

Clarke, H. Harrison, *Application of Measurement to Health and Physical Education*, Fourth Edition. Englewood Cliffs, N.J.: Prentice-Hall, Inc., 1967.

Emery, Curtis Ray, *Modern Volleyball*. New York: The Macmillan Company, 1953.

Keller, Val, *Point, Game, and Match!* Hollywood, California: Creative Sports Books, P. O. Box 2244, 1968.

Laveaga, Robert E., *Volleyball*, Second Edition. New York: The Ronald Press Company, 1960.

Mathore, Marcel, *Technique du volleyball moderne*. Paris: Fédération Française de Volley-ball, 1964.

_____, *Le Guide de l'Entraineur*. Paris: Fédération Française de Volley-ball, 1965.

Trotter, Betty Jane, *Volleyball for Girls and Women*. New York: The Ronald Press Company, 1965.

Van Dalen, Deobold B., Mitchell, Elmer D., and Bennett, Bruce L., *A World History of Physical Education*. New York: Prentice-Hall, Inc., 1953.

Wardale, Peter, *Volleyball: Skills and Tactics*. London: Faber and Faber Limited, 24 Russell Square, 1964. Available in the U.S. from Sportshelf, P. O. Box 634, New Rochelle, N.Y.

Welch, J. Edmund, ed., *How to Play and Teach Volleyball*, First Edition. New York: Association Press, 1960.

HANDBOOKS AND MANUALS

Barnes, Mildred J., *Officiating DGWS Volleyball Rules*. Minneapolis: Burgess Publishing Company, 1965.

Boyden, E. Douglas, Burton, Roger G., and Odeneal, William T., *Volleyball Syllabus*. Pacific Palisades, California: P. O. Box 514, c/o Betty Ghormley, 1961.

Bratton, Robert D., ed., *1965 Canadian Volleyball Annual and Rule Book*. Scarborough, Ontario, Canada: CVA Publications, 78 Tedford Drive.

_____, *Power Volleyball for Player, Teacher, and Coach.* Scarborough, Ontario, Canada: CVA Publications, 78 Tedford Drive, 1968.

Chapman, Nancy L., ed., *1967-69 Volleyball Guide.* The Division for Girls' and Women's Sports, 1201 Sixteenth St., N.W., Washington, D.C.

Cohen, Harlan, *Power Volleyball Drills.* Hollywood, California: Creative Sports Books, P. O. Box 2244, 1966.

Engstrom, Glen H., and Schaafsma, Frances, *Volleyball.* Dubuque, Iowa: Wm. C. Brown Company Publishers, 1966.

Friermood, Harold T., ed., *Volleyball Skills Program for Olympic Development.* Sponsored by U.S. Olympic Committee and U.S. Volleyball Association, 1966, revised 1967. Available from USVBA Commissioner of Regions, 13 State Street, Schenectady, New York.

_____, *When Volleyball Began—An Olympic Sport,* 1966. New York: USVBA Secretary, 224 East 47th Street.

Furlani, Anton H., ed., *1968-69 Canadian Volleyball Annual and Rule Book.* Scarborough, Ontario, Canada: CVA Publications, 78 Tedford Drive.

_____, *1967-68 Canadian Volleyball Annual and Rule Book.* Scarborough, Ontario, Canada: CVA Publications, 78 Tedford Drive.

_____. *1966 Canadian Volleyball Annual and Rule Book.* Scarborough, Ontario, Canada: CVA Publications, 78 Tedford Drive.

Liba, Marie R., ed., *1963-65 Volleyball Guide.* The Division for Girls' and Women's Sports, 1201 Sixteenth St., N.W., Washington, D.C.

Lockhart, Aileene, ed., *Selected Volleyball Articles.* The Division for Girls' and Women's Sports, 1201 Sixteenth St., N.W., Washington, D.C., 1959.

Marshall, Sol H., *Capsule History of Volleyball.* Hollywood, California: Creative Sports Books, P. O. Box 2244, 1968.

McGown, Carl M., ed., *It's Power Volleyball.* Pacific Palisades, California: P. O. Box 514, c/o Betty Ghormley, 1968.

Mott, Jane A., *Conditioning for Women.* Dubuque, Iowa: Wm. C. Brown Company Publishers, 1966.

Odeneal, William T., and Wilson, Harry E., *Beginning Volleyball,* First Edition. Belmont, California: Wadsworth Publishing Company, 1962.

Odeneal, William T., Wilson, Harry E., and Kellam, Mary Frances, *Beginning Volleyball,* Second Edition. Belmont, California: Wadsworth Publishing Company, 1969.

Official Volleyball Scorebook. The Division for Girls' and Women's Sports, 1201 Sixteenth St., N.W., Washington, D.C.

Pictorial Volleyball. Hollywood, California: Creative Sports Books, P. O. Box 2244, 1966.

Proceedings, Fourth National Institute on Girls' Sports. The Division for Girls' and Women's Sports, 1201 Sixteenth St., N.W., Washington, D.C., 1968.

Ricci, Benjamin, *Physical & Physiological Conditioning for Men.* Dubuque, Iowa: Wm. C. Brown Company Publishers, 1966.

Thigpen, Janet, *Power Volleyball for Girls and Women.* Dubuque, Iowa: Wm. C. Brown Company Publishers, 1967.

Tom, Marilyn C., and Luckman, Margaret N., *Coed Volleyball.* Palo Alto, California: The National Press, 1966.

Volleyball Scorebook. Berne, Ind.: USVBA Printer, P. O. Box 109.

Walters, Marshall L., ed., *1969 Official Volleyball Guide.* Berne, Ind.: USVBA Printer, P. O. Box 109.

_____, *1968 Official Volleyball Guide*. Berne, Ind.: USVBA Printer, P. O. Box 109.

_____, *1967 Official Volleyball Guide*. Berne, Ind.: USVBA Printer, P. O. Box 109.

_____, *1966 Official Volleyball Guide*. Berne, Ind.: USVBA Printer, P. O. Box 109.

_____, *1965 Official Volleyball Guide*. Berne, Ind.: USVBA Printer, P. O. Box 109.

Wills, Betty Jane, ed., *1965-67 Volleyball Guide*. The Division for Girls' and Women's Sports, 1201 Sixteenth St., N.W., Washington, D.C.

PERIODICAL ARTICLES

Alekseev, Evgueni, "Breaking the Defence," *International Volleyball Review*, April-May, 1968, p. 47.

Baley, James A., "Teaching the Spike in Volleyball," *Journal of Health, Physical Education, Recreation*, Nov.-Dec., 1964, p. 57.

Barta, Joe, "Fairest Foul of Them All," *Journal of Physical Education*, September-October, 1960, p. 17.

Boslooper, Thomas, "The Ideal Woman: Fit and Feminine," *Journal of Physical Education*, March-April, 1968, p. 99.

Brady, George F., "Preliminary Investigation of Volleyball Playing Ability," *Research Quarterly*, March, 1945, p. 14.

Burton, Roger, "Honor and the Silent Sound," *International Volleyball Review*, June-August, 1967, p. 74.

_____, "Coast Sweeps Play in Ioway," *International Volleyball Review*, May-June, 1959, p. 49.

Bush, Wayne L., "Volleyball Drills for the Gym Class and Varsity Squad," *Journal of Physical Education*, May-June, 1950, p. 104.

Butler, Willie Mae, "Comparison of Two Methods of Measuring the Degree of Skill in the Underarm Volleyball Serve," *Research Quarterly*, May, 1961, p. 261.

Clifton, Marguerite A., "Single Hit Volley Test for Women's Volleyball," *Research Quarterly*, May, 1962, p. 208.

Coleman, Jim, "Coaches Corner," *International Volleyball Review*, March-April, 1966, p. 42.

_____, "The World's Cup," *International Volleyball Review*, March-April, 1966, p. 30.

_____, "USSR vs USA in Canada," *International Volleyball Review*, December, 1965-January, 1966, p. 5.

Cunningham, Phyllis, and Garrison, Joan. "High Wall Test for Women's Volleyball," *Research Quarterly*, October, 1968, p. 486.

Davies, Glen, "Impressions of Olympic Volleyball," *Journal of Physical Education*, Jan.-Feb., 1965, p. 78.

Doherty, John P., "Old Volleyballs Never Die," *The Physical Educator*, May, 1968, p. 87.

Friermood, Harold T., "In Memoriam-Idell and Laveaga," *Journal of Physical Education*, July-August, 1966, p. 147.

_____, "The Olympic Games," *Journal of Physical Education*, Jan.-Feb., 1965, p. 51.

_____, "Tribute to A. Provost Idell," *International Volleyball Review*, November-December, 1966, p. 8.

_____, "Volleyball Goes Modern!" *Journal of Health, Physical Education, Recreation,* May, 1953, p. 10.

Garrett, Leon, Sabie, Mohammed, and Pangle, Roy, "Four Approaches to Increasing Cardiovascular Fitness during Volleyball Instruction," *Research Quarterly,* December, 1965, p. 496.

Geisler, Fred W., "Volleyball," *Journal of Health, Physical Education, Recreation,* January, 1966, p. 31.

Hooks, Edgar W., Jr., "Hooks' Comprehensive Knowledge Test in Selected Physical Education Activities for College Men," *Research Quarterly,* December, 1966, p. 506.

Jensen, Clayne R., and Dotson, Larry, "An Analysis of Serving Methods in Volleyball," *Athletic Journal,* Mar., 1966, p. 34.

Keiser, Helen E., "Volleyball Circuit Training," *The Physical Educator,* May, 1967, p. 69.

Kronqvist, Roger A., and Brumbach, Wayne B., "A Modification of the Brady Volleyball Skill Test for High School Boys," *Research Quarterly,* March, 1968, p. 116.

Layman, Richard, "The Most Abused Exercise" (deep knee bend), *Journal of Physical Education,* November-December, 1966, p. 41.

Leibrock, Philip, "Volleyball the Right Way," *Scholastic Coach,* December, 1965, p. 30.

Ley, Katherine, "DGWS National Intercollegiate Athletic Championships for Women," *Journal of Health, Physical Education, Recreation,* February, 1968, p. 24.

Liba, Marie R., and Stauff, Marilyn, R., "A Test for the Volleyball Pass," *Research Quarterly,* March, 1963, p. 56.

Lowell, John C., "Increasing the Zone of Effectiveness," *International Volleyball Review,* November-December, 1966, p. 14.

_____, "International Blocking, An Offensive Weapon," *International Volleyball Review,* November-December, 1966, p. 8.

_____, "Jump Training Outline," *International Volleyball Review,* Nov.-Dec., 1967, p. 9.

_____, "Pre-Olympic Trial Conditioning," *International Volleyball Review,* April-May, 1968, p. 43.

_____, "Techniques—Spiking in International Volleyball," *International Volleyball Review,* February-March, 1967, p. 33.

_____, "U.S. Men's Volleyball Team Wins Pan Am Title," *International Volleyball Review,* Nov.-Dec., 1967, p. 4.

_____, "Volleyball Training Hints—Jump & Bump to Win," *International Volleyball Review,* December, 1965-January, 1966, p. 15.

McManama, Jerre, and Shondell, Don, "Teaching Volleyball Fundamentals," *Journal of Health, Physical Education, Recreation,* March, 1969, p. 43.

Marsenach, Jacky, "Championnats du Monde de Volley-ball," *Revue Education Physique et Sports,* Paris, Novembre, 1966.

Marshall, Sol H., "Colleges Hold Key to U.S. Volleyball Success," *Amateur Athlete,* May, 1967, p. 16.

McVicar, J. W., "Fitness in Volleyball," *Journal of Physical Education,* July-August, 1962, p. 131.

Miller, C. L. Bobb, "Who Needs the Honor Call?" *Journal of Physical Education,* May-June, 1968, p. 139.

Mohr, Dorothy R., and Haverstick, Martha J., "Relationship Between Height, Jumping Ability, and Agility to Volleyball Skill," *Research Quarterly,* March, 1956, p. 74.

Nelson, Richard C., "Follow-up Investigation of the Velocity of the Volleyball Spike," *Research Quarterly,* Mar., 1964, p. 83.

Nemeth, Delphine, "Jane Ward Visits South Bend," *International Volleyball Review,* November-December, 1967, p. 15.

Odeneal, William T., "Competitive Volleyball Basics," *Scholastic Coach,* October, 1962, p. 57.

_____, "Offensive Volleyball," *Scholastic Coach,* November, 1954, p. 38.

_____, "What Ails U. S. Volleyball?" *Amateur Athlete,* April, 1965, p. 14.

"Official Bulletin of International Volleyball Federation," *The Spiker* (official news bulletin of Canadian Volleyball Association), February 7, 1967.

"Official Directives from the International Volleyball Federation and from Bobb Miller, USVBA Chairman of Officials," *International Volleyball Review,* November-December, 1966, p. 2.

Otott, Major George E., "Circuit (Power) Training," *Sport International,* No. 35/E, 1967, p. 14. Available from CISM, 119, avenue Franklin Roosevelt, Brussels 5, Belgium.

Peck, W. H., "U. S. Volleyball Championships—1965 Edition," *Journal of Physical Education,* July-August, 1965, p. 142.

Ronberg, Gary, "Playing It the Japanese Way," *Sports Illustrated,* June 5, 1967.

Ryan, Allan J., "Smoking and Health," *Journal of the Canadian Association for Health, Physical Education, and Recreation,* April-May, 1967, p. 32.

Scates, Allen E., "A Participating Player's Observations of the World Championships," *International Volleyball Review,* November-December, 1966, p. 6.

Shondell, Don, "Honor Call—Asset or Liability?" *International Volleyball Review,* June-August, 1967, p. 72. Also published in *1968 Official Volleyball Guide* (Berne, Indiana: USVBA Printer), pp. 119-120.

Singer, Robert N., "Sequential Skill Learning and Retention Effects in Volleyball," *Research Quarterly,* March, 1968, p. 185.

Warner, Richard C., "Pan Am Report," *Journal of Physical Education,* January-February, 1968, p. 83.

Watman, Thomas J., "Point Getting in Volleyball," *Athletic Journal,* Jan., 1965, p. 38.

Welch, J. Edmund, "First Volleyball Camp in U. S. A.," *Journal of Physical Education,* September-October, 1968, pp. 18-19.

_____, "The Set in Volleyball," *Coach & Athlete,* December, 1968, p. 14.

_____, "International Variations in Volleyball Officiating," *Journal of Physical Education,* January-February, 1968, p. 86. Also published in *International Volleyball Review,* April-May, 1968, p. 48.

_____, "Prospects of the United States Volleyball Team in the 1964 Olympic Games," *The Physical Educator,* May, 1963, p. 61.

_____, "Volleyball Chest Pass Is Dead?" *Athletic Journal,* December, 1967, p. 24.

Whitehead, E., "Kaizuka Nichibo Women's Volleyball Team . . . 'Driven beyond Dignity,'" *Sports Illustrated,* Mar. 16, 1964, p. 16.

Wilson, Harry E., "Fresno Wins National Men's Open Championships," *International Volleyball Review,* June-August, 1967, p. 59.

_____, "Notes," *International Volleyball Review,* February-March, 1967, p. 31.

MAGAZINES

Bulletin Officiel, International Volleyball Federation, Bld. Tolboukhine 18, Sofia, Bulgaria.

International Volleyball Review, P. O. Box 554, Encino, Calif.

The Spiker, Canadian Volleyball Association, 78 Tedford Drive, Scarborough 4, Ontario, Canada.

FILMS

Introducing Volleyball, CVA Publications, 78 Tedford Dr., Scarborough 4, Ont., Canada. (Filmstrips or slides—color).

Olympic Volleyball Films, 1964. Hollywood, California: Volleyball National Information Center, P. O. Box 1264. (Motion picture—black and white, silent).

Power Volleyball, 1968. Chicago: The Athletic Institute, 805 Merchandise Mart. (Loop films—color).

Power Volleyball—The Story of the National Tournament, 1966. Hollywood, California: Volleyball National Information Center, P. O. Box 1264. (Motion picture—color, sound).

USA vs Russia, 1965. Roger G. Burton, 100 Gibbs Street, Rochester, New York. (Motion picture—color, silent).

Volleyball Drills and Techniques, All-American Productions and Publishers, Box 2201, Tuscaloosa, Ala. (Motion picture—color or black and white, sound).

Volleyball for Women, All-American Productions and Publishers, Box 2201, Tuscaloosa, Ala. 35401. (Motion picture—color or black and white, sound).

PROGRAMS

Official Program, 5th Pan American Games Volleyball Championships, Winnipeg, Canada, 1967.

Official Program, YMCA-USVBA National Volleyball Championships, Portland, Oregon, 1968.

OLYMPIC GAMES AND PAN AMERICAN GAMES MATERIALS

Fifth Pan-American Games Official Guide, 1967. Cambridge Publishers, 305 Broadway, Winnipeg, Manitoba, Canada.

Olympiad 1960. Italian State Tourist Department, Rome, Italy.

Olympic Pictorial—1967 United States Pan-American Team Handbook. United States Olympic Committee, New York, New York.

Olympic Sports—Volleyball, 1962. United States Olympic Committee, New York, New York.

XVIII Olympiad, 1964. Asahi Broadcasting Corporation, Tokyo, Japan.

Olympics '68. ABC TV Sports Guidebook, A Rutledge Book, The Benjamin Company, 485 Madison Avenue, New York, New York.

The Olympic Games—Fundamental Principles, Rules and Regulations, General Information, 1962. International Olympic Committee, Champagne Mon-Repos, Lausanne, Switzerland.

The Sports Illustrated Book of the Olympic Games, 1968. Time-Life Books, New York, New York.

UNPUBLISHED MATERIALS

Davis, Patricia A., "A Manual for Teaching Attack Volleyball to High School Students and Beginners" (unpublished M.Ed. thesis, University of North Carolina, Greensboro, North Carolina, 1966).

Jensen, Judith L., "The History and Development of Volleyball for Girls and Women" (unpublished M.S. thesis, Ohio State University, Columbus, Ohio, 1959).

Lowell, John C., "Volleyball as a Combative Sport" (unpublished syllabus, The Church College of Hawaii, Laie, Hawaii, 1967).

_____, "Volleyball Skill Test for College Men" (unpublished M.S. thesis, Brigham Young University, Provo, Utah, 1965).

Lu, Hui-Ching, "An Analysis of Volleyball in Various Regions of the World" (unpublished Ed.D. dissertation, Teacher's College, Columbia University, New York, New York, 1950). Condensation published by *International Volleyball Review*, 1950.

McGown, Carl M., "Reflections of a Journey" (unpublished report of study in Poland and at 1966 World Volleyball Championships, The Church College of Hawaii, Laie, Hawaii, 1966).

Odeneal, William T., "The History and Contributions of the United States Volleyball Association" (unpublished D.P.E. dissertation, Springfield College, Springfield, Massachusetts, 1968).

Shondell, Donald S., "The Relationship of Selected Motor and Anthropometric Traits to Successful Volleyball Performance" (unpublished P.E.D. dissertation, Indiana University, Bloomington, Indiana, 1969).

Tiidus, Arvo, "The Physical Fitness Status of the Canadian 1959 and 1963 Pan American Volleyball Teams" (unpublished M.S. thesis, University of Illinois, Champaign, Illinois, 1964).

Unpublished notebook, Columbus YMCA Volleyball Camp, Bellefontaine, Ohio, 1968.

INFORMATION CENTER

Volleyball National Information Center, P. O. Box 1264, Hollywood, Calif. 90028. (Teaching and coaching aids, films, manuals, photographs, volleyball records).

Appendix A

POWER VOLLEYBALL—This level of volleyball differs from recreational volleyball in the amount of organization necessary for the highly refined application of team strategy and individual skills. Power volleyball demands a quick and alert, extremely well-coordinated athlete, with great stamina to master its complex skills and playing situations.

OFFENSE—The action by a team controlling the ball. It includes reception of the serve, setting, and attacking the ball. The serve is also an offensive action.

DEFENSE—The action by a team when the ball is controlled by its opponents. Defense pertains primarily to tactics employed by the serving team.

SERVE—The method in which the ball is put into play by hitting it with any part of the hand, fist, or forearm, over the net and into the opponents' court.

PASS—The controlled movement of the ball from one player to another on the same team.

OVERHAND PASS—A ball played with the fingertips of both hands. Contact is made in front of the face, and the ball is usually passed in the direction in which the player is facing.

*FOREARM PASS—A ball played in an underhand manner. The forearms, held away from the body, will act as a surface from which the pass can be made.

**SET—A pass, made overhand or underhand, hit into the air for the purpose of placing the ball in position for the attack.

---

* In referring to the FOREARM PASS in this text, the editor has chosen to use these terms—DOUBLE FOREARM PASS and SINGLE FOREARM PASS.

** In defining the SET, the national coaches refer to a pass made overhand or underhand. By underhand, they mean with a forearm pass or a one-hand dig. They do not mean with both palms turned upward. The coaches also use the term, ATTACK. A more common term for this action is SPIKE.

ATTACK—The act of jumping in the air and hitting a set ball from above the level of the net into the opponents' court.

BLOCK—A defensive play by one or more players who attempt to intercept the ball near the net.

DIG—Recovery of an opponents' attack, made by playing the ball with one or two hands.

DIVE AND ROLL—Techniques employed to increase the player's range of effectiveness, especially on defense.

Appendix B

BULLETIN OFFICIEL D'INFORMATIONS
International Volleyball Federation

FÉDÉRATION INTERNATIONALE DE VOLLEYBALL
International VolleyBall Federation
23, RUE D'ANJOU - PARIS 8ᵉ (FRANCE)

FIVB

BULLETIN OFFICIEL D'INFORMATIONS

MOTION

LAID DOWN BY THE RULES OF THE GAME COMMITTEE AND THE
INTERNATIONAL ARBITRATION COMMITTEE FOLLOWING THE UNA-
NIMOUS REQUEST OF THE MEMBERS OF THE IVBF CONGRESS

The 10th Congress of IVBF, which met in Praha, 8-10
September 1966, in the interest of Volleyball for the future,
adopted a resolution that is to be passed on to all National
Federations concerning the role of Officials and their interpretation of the touch of the ball, particularly the receiving
of the service as well as all other play.

The present "hard officiating" is not the intent of
Volleyball and IVBF is concerned that the game remains as originated and not to be transformed into another type of game.

The practise of touching the ball with the fingers, as
opposed to the closed fist underhand hit, has been the essen-
ce of Volleyball from the beginning. "Hard officiating" has a
tendency to force players to deviate from the original methods
of play and adopt practices which tend to change the game.
However, IVBF does not object to the closed fist underhand hit,
which has its place in the game.

The IVBF strongly insists that all National Federations
instruct their technical Committees, officials, coaches, etc..
to give their attention to the technique of playing the ball
with the fingers and assuring that officials are permitting
proper play of the ball, according to the Rules of the Game.

The INTERNATIONAL ARBITRATION COMMITTEE OF IVBF is responsible to see that this resolution is carried out during all
official international competition.

Reproduced from *The Spiker,* Official News Bulletin of the Canadian Volleyball Association, February 7, 1967, p. 11.

Appendix C

HOOKS' VOLLEYBALL EXAMINATION[1]

Statistical Validity was done by Item Analysis with an Index of Discrimination Range from .23 to .79 and a Level of Difficulty Range from .23 to .90. All responses are functional at the 2 percent level of selection. Reliability is .81 as determined by test-retest. National and AAHPER District Percentile Norms are based upon 4,140 subjects. Individuals desiring to order copies of the examination and instructor's manuals, including answer keys, may write to: Dr. Edgar W. Hooks, Jr., Professor of Physical Education, Box 2745, Greenville, North Carolina 27834.

1. In what country was volleyball first played?
   A. Canada   B. Denmark   C. England   D. United States
2. What was the first name given to volleyball?
   A. Handball   B. Mintonette   C. Poona   D. Shuttlenet   E. Volleyball
3. Which hit does the setter usually make?
   A. First   B. Second   C. Third
4. Which of the following qualities would be of *least* concern in choosing a setter?
   A. Competitive spirit   B. Mental alertness   C. Size   D. Speed
5. What is the primary difficulty with a serve to the extreme rear of the opponent's court?
   A. It is hard to hit the ball that distance.   B. It often goes beyond the end line.   C. Only an overhand service can be used to gain the needed power.
   D. The angle of descent makes it easy to pass the ball back to the front court.
6. What kind of ball was used in the first volleyball games?
   A. A basketball   B. The bladder of a basketball   C. The bladder of a soccer ball   D. A soccer ball   E. A playground ball
7. On which of the following plays would holding the ball be most likely to occur?
   A. Overhand pass from the back-court area   B. Clenched-fist underhand pass on a ball near the floor   C. Set near the net   D. Two-hand underhand pass with the palms turned up
8. What is the primary purpose of a recovery shot?
   A. To hit the ball high enough to permit a teammate to make a good set or placement   B. To keep the opposing team from scoring   C. To recover the serve   D. To score a point through the use of an effective shot

---

[1] This knowledge test was part of a dissertation done by Edgar W. Hooks, Jr., at George Peabody College for Teachers in 1964. Where necessary, questions have been revised to conform to the 1969 USVBA Rules.

9. Which of the following is *incorrect* for the right-handed underhand serve?
A. The feet are parallel with the toes equidistant from the end line. B. The ball is held in the palm and fingers of the left hand. C. The knees are slightly flexed. D. The body pivots to the right as the right arm is swung backward. E. The right arm follows through in a forward and upward direction.

10. What is the score of a forfeited game?
A. 1-0 B. 3-0 C. 7-0 D. 11-0 E. 15-0

11. What decision should be made when opposing players contact the ball simultaneously above the net and it falls out of bounds on the receiving team's side?
A. The point should be played over. B. A point should be awarded to the serving team. C. Side out should be declared.

12. Which of the following would reduce the effectiveness of a defensive player who is waiting to receive the ball?
A. Body flexed at the waist B. Feet comfortably spread C. Hands and arms held by the sides at hip level D. Knees flexed E. One foot slightly in front of the other

13. What is the official length for a volleyball net?
A. 28 feet B. 29 feet C. 30 feet D. 31 feet E. 32 feet

14. What is the maximum number of substitutions that a team may make per game?
A. 6 B. 8 C. 10 D. 12 E. 14

15. What position should the best spiker play when his team starts a game by serving to the opposing team?
A. Left forward B. Center forward C. Right forward D. Right back E. Left back

16. What is the time limit for the completion of a game, provided that one team has a two-point advantage?
A. 5 minutes B. 7 minutes C. 8 minutes D. 10 minutes E. 12 minutes

17. For college men, what is the net height at the center of the court?
A. 7 feet B. 7 feet 3 inches C. 7 feet 6 inches D. 8 feet E. 8 feet 6 inches

18. Which of the following is the most effective method of passing the volleyball?
A. Overhand pass B. Dig pass C. Forearm pass D. One-hand pass E. Two-hand underhand pass

19. Which of the following solutions would be acceptable when the service area behind the end line is too small to permit enough space for serving?
A. The service area is extended into the court far enough to provide adequate serving space. B. The server may step on the end line but not into the court in the act of serving. C. The server must serve in the small area that exists. D. The server may serve from beyond the end of the end line and take a step along the side boundary line. E. The service area is extended to the rear spiker's line.

20. Which of the following would be illegal during the service?
A. The server fails to keep both feet in contact with the floor while serving. B. The server puts the ball in play by hitting it with his arm. C. The server runs back and forth along the end line before hitting the ball. D. The server bounces the ball quickly, catches it, and then serves.

21. What body parts are used to contact the ball on an overhand pass?
A. Clenched fists B. Fleshy parts of the fingers and thumbs C. Heels of the hands D. Palms of the hands E. Wrists

183

22. Which of the following would be good spiking strategy?
A. Contact the ball at the top of the net in order to score several points on net balls. B. Get as close to the net as you can before jumping to spike the ball. C. Spike most balls diagonally across the court. D. Spike most balls straight down the court. E. Spike with very little follow-through in order not to hit the net.

23. Which of the following applies to a one-man block?
A. Best defense against a spike B. Best results when it is used on the right or left side of the court C. Better than a two-man block because no teamwork is required D. More effective when one hand is placed on the back of the other hand in order to bring the arms closer together E. Not too effective against a good spiker

24. What is a multiple block?
A. A ball which is blocked on one side of the net and then blocked on the other side of the net before a point is scored or side out is called B. A block in which one player blocks a ball and has the ball rebound off his hands against some other part of the body C. A block in which the ball touches both of the blocker's hands above the net D. A block in which two opponents strike the ball simultaneously and directly over the net E. A block in which two or more players team up to block a spike and make only one attempt to play the ball

25. Which player is usually the quarterback or director of team play on a volleyball team?
A. Blocker B. Passer C. Server D. Setter E. Spiker

26. What are volleyball standards?
A. Devices to which the net is attached B. Regulations concerning the dimensions of a volleyball court C. Regulations governing the execution of fundamental skills D. Rules regulating play E. Rules to follow in developing strategy

27. Which of the following factors is the most important in a good offense?
A. Ability to follow accepted strategy B. Ability to jump C. Ability to pass and set D. Ability to recover good placements E. Ability to spike

28. How much time is a team allotted for a time-out?
A. 30 seconds B. one minute C. 1½ minutes D. two minutes

29. What is an ace?
A. An outstanding volleyball player B. A spike hit so hard that it cannot be returned C. A game in which one team does not score any points D. A spike that is not touched by an opponent before it strikes the floor E. A serve hit so the defense cannot return it

30. In preparing to spike, where should the ball be in relation to the hitting shoulder?
A. About one foot to the left of it B. About one foot to the right of it C. About three feet above and slightly behind it D. About three feet directly over it E. Out in front and in a direct line of flight with it.

31. What is the length of the rest period between games of a match?
A. 1 minute B. 2 minutes C. 3 minutes D. 4 minutes E. 5 minutes

32. In what area of the court are the majority of the serves placed?
A. Across the back seven and one-half feet of the court B. Across the center fifteen feet of the court C. Across the forward seven and one-half feet of the court D. In the left front quarter of the court E. In the right front quarter of the court

33. Which of the following persons may *not* make a request for a time-out for his team?
A. Player   B. Captain   C. Manager   D. Coach

34. What is the best strategy against a team that has no weak ball handlers?
A. Always play the ball three times on your side of the net   B. Hit every shot hard   C. Hit high lobs to the back-court area   D. Hit the ball between the players   E. Hit the ball directly at the players

35. From what area may the server put the ball into play?
A. Any point behind the end line   B. Only behind the right one third of the end line   C. Only behind the center twenty feet of the end line   D. Only behind the right one half of the end line

36. Which of the following would be a violation in returning the ball across the net?
A. Player "A-1" spikes a ball that strikes the top of the net and forces the net under player "B-1's" arm   B. Player "B-1" strikes the ball with the wrist instead of the hand on an attempted spike   C. Player "A-1" returns the ball after a simultaneous contact by players "A-1" and "A-2"   D. Player "A-1" crosses the imaginary extension of the center line and plays the ball back to a teammate.

37. In which of the following situations would there be *no* foul on the part of the server?
A. A served ball touches a teammate before crossing the net and falling into the opposing team's court.   B. A served ball touches the net and falls into the opposing team's court.   C. A served ball touches the net post and falls into the opposing team's court.   D. The server kicks the ball over the net and it falls into the opposing team's court.   E. The server throws the ball into the air and with both hands hits it over the net.

38. Which of the following determines the completion of a play in which the referee is watching for a foul?
A. When each player regains his equilibrium and physical control   B. When the ball crosses the net   C. When the ball strikes the floor   D. When the ball is hit the first time after it crosses the net   E. When the ball is contacted by the player who hits it over the net

39. Which of the following is a foul?
A. The ball is hit and passes over the side-line tape on the net   B. The center back serves the ball   C. The server stands with the upper part of his body leaning over the end line prior to starting the serve   D. The server swings his arm over the end line before contacting the ball

40. Which of the following actions constitutes a foul by a player?
A. Following through over the net after a spike   B. Making successive contacts of the ball when playing a hard-driven spiked ball   C. Being part of a three-man block   D. Screening of a serve

41. In which of the following plays is a foot fault most likely to occur?
A. A pass from back court   B. A pass from out-of-bounds   C. A serve   D. A set near the ten-foot spiking line   E. A spike near the ten-foot spiking line

42. Which of the following techniques would contribute *very little* to the overhand serve?
A. Ball tossed above the head   B. Ball tossed slightly in front of the right arm and shoulder   C. Elbow bent on the forward swing   D. Ball hit with the heel of the hand   E. Follow-through down and across the body

43. When may a player make successive contacts with the ball?
A. On a floating serve   B. On a multiple block   C. On a net recovery

D. On an attempt to return the ball from out-of-bounds   E. On an attempt to spike from behind the rear spiker's line

44. Which of the following is the first essential in offensive strategy?
A. Pass   B. Recovery   C. Spike   D. Serve   E. Set

45. Which of the following would be *incorrect* when making an overhand pass?
A. Arms extended upward   B. Elbows close by the sides   C. Fingers comfortably spread   D. Palms turned outward toward the ball   E. Thumbs turned in and close together

46. Which of the following would be *incorrect* in playing a net ball?
A. Turn one side toward the net   B. Assume a stride stance   C. Crouch and wait for the ball   D. Play the ball as soon as it leaves the net   E. Play the ball with clenched fists, wrists, or forearms

47. Which of the following would make a blocker *less* effective in executing a good block?
A. Pushing the arms and hands forward as the block is made   B. Jumping with the body straight up and down and close to the net   C. Placing the wrists in line with and just above the net   D. Taking off by springing with both feet   E. Tilting the arms forward and close to the net before the block is made

48. Which of the following would be *poor* strategy in spiking?
A. Drive each spike with a vicious swing   B. Drive the ball towards the side lines   C. Hit the ball at various angles   D. "Dink" the ball over the blockers' hands   E. Use the same arm and body motion on each spiking approach

49. Which of the following formations would be best for receiving the service?
A. Front-line players at the rear of their areas and back-line players near the front of their areas   B. Front-line players at the rear of their areas and back-line players near the rear of their areas   C. Front-line players near net and back-line players near the front of their areas   D. Front-line players near the center of their areas and back-line players at the rear of their areas   E. Front-line players near the net and back-line players at the rear of their areas

50. Which of the following is the initial key to playing successful volleyball?
A. Blocking   B. Passing   C. Setting   D. Spiking

Appendix D

INTERNATIONAL RULES INTERPRETATIONS*

1. The size of the court is 30 feet by 60 feet. The net height for men is 8 feet and for women 7 feet 4¼ inches.
2. A team may have a total of 12 players, but only six are allowed on the court at any one time. Substitutions may be made during the game.
3. International matches consist of three out of five games. The team first scoring 15 points with an advantage of two points wins the game.
4. A team shall score a point each time they serve the ball, if the opponents fail to return the ball back over the net in a manner allowed by the rules.
5. A team is allowed one, two or three hits to play the ball back into the opponents' court.
6. After each loss of serve, the team which is to serve, must rotate one position to their right.
7. Each team is allowed two timeouts during each game. A timeout consists of 30 seconds.
8. A player may hit the ball with any part of the body above the waist.
9. The ball when it passes over the net above or between the court sidelines is good and in play.
10. The ball must touch the floor within the court or touch any part of the line to be good in play.
11. A player cannot touch the ball more than once, but may play the ball a second time providing a team player has touched the ball.
12. The ball cannot come to rest momentarily in the hands of a player. Lifting, scooping, pushing, or carrying the ball is prohibited.
13. A player may not touch the net at any time.
14. A player may not step over the court centre line.
15. An offensive player must hit the ball from his own side of the net.
16. A defensive player may block the ball with his hands over the net providing he allows the attacker to hit the ball first.
17. A back line player may not attack a ball from above the height of the net into the opponents' court when playing the ball from within ten feet of the net.
18. A player may not make personal or derogatory remarks to an official or opponent.
19. A player may not stamp his feet or make any other distracting gesture towards an opponent.
20. A team may not receive instructions from a coach, manager, or substitute from outside the court.
21. The captain is the only player on the court who may address the officials.
22. The referee's decisions are final.

---

* *Official Program*, 5th Pan American Games, Winnipeg, Canada, 1967, p. 6.

These are abbreviated rules interpretations only. For example, in Interpretation #11, a player in the act of blocking may touch the ball twice. A complete set of International Rules may be found in the *Canadian Volleyball Annual and Rule Book*, 78 Tedford Drive, Scarborough, Ontario, Canada.

INDEX OF NAMES

Alekseev, Evgueni, 98, 173
Alstrom, John, 118, 119
Anthony, Don 38, 44, 171

Baley, James A., 79, 173
Barnes, Mildred J., 170, 171
Barta, Joe, 33, 173
Batchelor, Harry A., 23
Bell, Mary M., 170
Bennett, Bruce L., 13, 171
Boslooper, Thomas, 124, 173
Boyden, E. Douglas, 10, 11, 25, 27, 28, 44, 46, 127, 171
Bozigian, Tom, 118
Brady, George F., 157, 158, 173
Bratton, Robert D., 44, 171, 172
Breitkreutz, Emil W., 28
Bridle, Wez, 16, 94
Bright, Mike, 60
Brown, Elwood S., 20, 79
Brown, Franklin H., 20
Brown, John, Jr., 21, 22, 23, 28
Brumbach, Wayne B., 157, 158, 174
Brundage, Avery, 23
Burroughs, W. P., 24
Burton, Roger G., 16, 25, 33, 44, 52, 54, 171, 173, 176
Bush, Wayne L., 158, 173
Butler, Willie Mae, 173

Caplan, Richard I., 27
Cardinal, Charles H., 79
Carroll, Irwin J., 142
Chambliss, Gene O., 16, 120, 124
Chapman, Nancy L., 172
Cherebetiu, Gabriel, 171
Clark, John K., 16
Clarke, H. Harrison, 158, 171
Clifton, Marguerite A., 157, 158, 172
Cobb, Ty, 77
Cohen, Harlan, 16, 52, 53, 93, 94, 118, 120, 121, 124, 152, 158, 172
Coleman, James E., 16, 26, 55, 63, 64, 91, 92, 98, 103, 111, 122, 124, 173
Creswell, George J., Jr., 16
Crocker, J. Howard, 20
Crockett, P. A., 124
Cubbon, Robert C., 20
Cunningham, Phyllis, 159, 173
Curran, J. J., 19

Danford, Howard G., 9, 11, 31
Davies, Glen, 16, 32, 33, 118, 124, 173
Davis, Patricia A., 159, 177
de Coubertin, Pierre, 13, 18

De Groot, E. B., Jr., 16, 23, 24, 27, 60, 63
Demachi, 55
Deweese, James C., Jr., 9, 35
Doherty, John P., 159, 173
Dotson, Larry, 44, 174
Duke, Horace "Smitty," 16
Dunlap, Ken, 16

Edmunds, Murrell, 9, 45
Eggert, Del, 124
Egstrom, Glen H., 61, 63, 172
Emery, Curtis Ray, 24, 158, 171
Engen, Rolf, 52, 118
Erikson, Keith, 121

Feely, Martin J., 16
Fish, Alton W., 28
Fisher, George J., 20, 21, 23, 24, 28, 29
Friermood, Harold T., 9, 11, 22, 23, 24, 25, 26, 28, 29, 33, 79, 159, 172, 173, 174
Furlani, Anton H., 16, 172

Garrett, Leon, 174
Garrison, Joan, 159, 173
Geisler, Fred W., 159, 174
Ghormley, Betty Ann, 16, 44, 54, 79, 171, 172
Gibson, Leonard C., 28
Gordon, David T., 22
Gray, J. H., 20
Griffith, John L., 16
Gulick, Luther Halsey, 19

Hagen, Hoadley, 16
Haine, Tom, 70
Halstead, Alfred T., 19
Hammer, Dick, 49
Hammersmith, Andrew A., 23
Harlowe, James, 15
Harris, Dorothy V., 170
Haverstick, Martha J., 157, 158, 174
Heisler, Edward A., 28
Henn, Jack, 95
Hooks, Edgar W., Jr., 16, 157, 158, 174, 182
Hrenchuk, Emil, 16
Hunt, Gayle, 116

Idell, A. Provost, 23, 24, 25, 113
Ignatio, Catalino R., 16

Jensen, Clayne R., 44, 174
Jensen, Judith L., 170, 177
Johnson, Dennis, 37

Kaczmarek, Len, 118
Keiser, Helen E., 159, 174
Kellam, Mary Frances, 11, 161, 172

Keller, Val, 16, 99, 111, 122, 171
Kennedy, Merton H., 24, 28
Knabe, Ernest W., 16
Kronqvist, Roger A., 157, 158, 174

Lang, Ronnie, 49, 52, 60, 119
Laveago, Robert E., 5, 22, 24, 29, 113, 170, 171
Layman, Richard, 124, 174
Leibrock, Philip, 54, 174
Lewis, Marshall, 75
Ley, Katherine, 174
Liba, Marie R., 157, 158, 172, 174
Litshauer, Ida C., 16
Little, Arthur D., 26
Lockhart, Aileene, 172
Lowell, John C., 10, 11, 52, 54, 64, 76, 78, 79, 86, 94, 98, 119, 122, 124, 125, 159, 174, 177
Lu, Hui-Ching, 24, 177
Lynch, John, 19
Luckman, Margaret N., 54, 172

Marsenach, Jacky, 174
Marshall, Sol H., 16, 122, 125, 172, 174
Mathore, Marcel, 171
Matiasek, Vaclav, 124
McDonald, G. R., 16, 118, 120, 122, 124
McDonough, Thomas E., Sr., 16
McGill, F. G., 23
McGowan, Carl M., 16, 52, 54, 74, 79, 111, 122, 123, 172, 177
McManama, Jerre, 16, 159, 174
McVicar, J. W., 125, 174
Medlin, C. H., Jr., 124
Meltzer, Peter S., 142
Miller, C. L. Bobb, 16, 33, 119, 124, 142, 174, 175
Mitchell, Elmer D., 13, 171
Mohr, Dorothy R., 157, 158, 174
Montague, Jim, 73
Morgan, William G., 18, 19, 22, 25, 29, 66
Morland, Richard B., 16
Morrison, Robert, 24, 28
Mott, Jane A., 125, 172
Mundt, Logan C., 24, 25, 29
Musica, Tony, 48

Naismith, James, 18
Nelson, Richard C., 10, 142, 143, 175
Nelson, Viggo O., 24, 25, 27, 28

Nemeth, Delphine, 64, 175
Nishikawa Masaichi, 24

Odeneal, William T., 10, 11, 26, 35, 44, 79, 81, 101, 111, 142 171, 172, 175, 177
O'Hara, Michael F., 10, 65, 121
Otott, George E., 125, 175

Pangle, Roy V., 5, 174
Pearson, George, 16
Peck, Wilbur H., 16, 28, 31, 33, 55, 63, 117, 124, 175
Perry, Barbara, 51, 97
Plotnick, B. A., 124
Poyerkof, 55
Pratt, Herbert L., 21, 23
Prsala, Jan, 16

Ricci, Benjamin, 125, 172
Robbins, C. C., 23, 74, 113
Rogers, James E., 25
Ronberg, Gary, 98, 175
Rule, Robert A., 16
Rundle, Larry, 63, 88, 119
Ryan, Allan, 125, 175
Ryan, Tom, 120

Sabie, Mohammed, 174
Savvin, Vladimir, 16, 46, 140, 142

Scates, Allen E., 16, 63, 73, 111, 120, 124, 125, 175
Scott, Larry, 49
Selznick, Eugene, 16, 49, 52, 58
Serantos, George, 118
Shaafsma, Frances, 61, 172
Shondell, Donald S., 16, 29, 33, 42, 44, 63, 64, 85, 98, 106, 111, 119, 124, 125, 159, 174, 175, 177
Singer, Robert N., 159, 175
Sivek, 55
Smith, Warren W., 16
Smyth, Donald, 16
Stagg, Amos Alonzo, 21
Stallcup, Leonard B., 3, 16
Stanley, Jon, 118, 119, 120
Stauff, Marilyn R., 157, 158, 174
Stewart, Andrew, 23

Thigpen, Janet, 172
Thomas, Royal L., 23
Tiidus, Arro, 125, 177
Tom, Marilynn C., 54, 172
Trotter, Betty Jane, 27, 47, 54, 171

Van Dalen, Deobold B., 13, 171

Velasco, Pete, 119
Vengierofski, 55

Walker, Albert V., 23
Walters, Marshall L., 9, 10, 11, 24, 26, 29, 54, 65, 142, 172, 173
Ward, Jane, 50, 64, 170
Wardale, Peter, 16, 35, 44, 49, 54, 65, 76, 79, 98, 127, 131, 142, 171
Warner, Richard C., 175
Watman, Thomas J., 96, 175
Watson, Mark, 16, 122
Watson, Thomas J., 23
Welch, Edith, 16
Welch, J. Edmund, 11, 25, 26, 29, 31, 45, 54, 55, 75, 81, 101, 140, 159, 171, 175
Whitehead E., 99, 175
Wickstrom, R. L., 159
Williams, Edward, 32
Wills, Betty Jane, 173
Wilson, Harry E., 16, 22, 26, 27, 35, 44, 46, 54, 96, 99, 111, 119, 122, 124, 172, 175
Wood, Frank, 19
Wortham, James, 25

Zimman, Harold O., 16

INDEX OF SUBJECTS

Amateur Athletic Union, 22
American Association for Health, Physical Education, and Recreation (AAHPER), 11, 15, 16, 22, 127, 161, 182
Armed Forces, 10, 20, 22, 23, 138
Athletic Institute, 24
Attack, definition, 180 (see Blocking, Serving, and Spiking), 47, 53, 65, 66, 67, 85, 101, 110, 152, 167; pass-set-spike (1-2-3), 63, 69, 167; spiking first ball, 63, 76, 155; spiking second ball, 72, 76, 77, 89, 106, 152; three-spiker attack, 15, 49, 84, 89, 92, 106, 107, 109, 110, 153, 154
Audio-visual aids, 23, 24, 27, 121, 139, 140, 143, 155

Ball handling (see Passing and Setting), 47, 48, 59, 77, 101, 128, 137, 146, 155
Bibliography, 17, 171-177
Blocking the ball, definition, 180, 47, 55, 56, 57, 61, 62, 66, 68, 69, 73, 74, 76, 81, 85-93, 101, 102, 103, 107, 109, 115, 118, 119, 120, 139, 140, 141, 144, 150, 151, 152, 154, 155, 167, 168; one-man block, 86, 107, 167; over-the-net block, 15, 63, 77, 78, 86, 110; supporting the block, 81, 91-93; three-man block, 85, 89, 167; two-man block, 86, 89, 152, 167

Canadian Volleyball Association (CVA), 15, 22, 44, 134, 136, 181
Captain, 102, 123, 131, 133, 135, 141; captain's insignia, 141
Class organization (see Teaching techniques), 143-144; balls, 144; drills, 154-156; net and supports, 155-156; score board, 156; syllabus, 10
Classifying players, 157
Clinics, 137-140
Coaches and coaching, 26, 27, 45, 56, 57, 81, 113, 117, 119, 120, 122, 123, 124, 133, 135, 139, 141, 143, 157, 161
Co-ed volleyball, 24, 144, 154, 161
Conditioning (see Training), 10, 57, 62, 66, 71, 72, 113-125, 144, 163-164, 165

Court (see Diagram, 34), 35, 137
Covering the spiker, 73, 81, 85-86, 104, 107

Defense, definition, 179, 15, 17, 45, 47, 52, 55, 57, 62, 76, 77, 78, 81-99, 102, 110, 111, 115, 118, 119, 120, 139, 150, 152, 154, 166; defending against the serve, 16, 45, 46, 49, 52-53, 81, 82, 83, 84, 85, 104, 108, 119, 130, 139, 141, 142, 164, 166-167; man back (white) defense, 91, 92; man up (red) defense, 91, 92; serve as a defensive weapon, 35, 36, 43
Diet, 114
Digging the ball, definition, 180, 45, 55, 77, 78, 81, 92, 93, 95, 96, 97, 98, 118, 119, 120, 147, 154, 155; out-of-the-net dig, 96-97; over-the-head dig, 96; with one hand, fist, or arm, 94, 96, 98, 162; with two arms (double forearm), 52-53, 98, 162
Dive and roll, 94, 110, 180; Japanese roll, 15, 53, 94, 97
Dive and save, 15, 52, 94, 95, 97
Dive and slide, 94, 119
Division for Girls' and Women's Sports (DGWS), 11, 15, 25, 127, 161, 169
Doubles volleyball, 154
Drills (see Power Volleyball Drills, Cohen, in Selected Bibliography, 172), 120, 123, 139, 143, 144, 148, 158; advanced drills, 152-154; blocking, 150; combination drills, 150-152; digging, 98, 147, 164-165; passing, 144, 145, 146, 147, 162-164; serving, 147-148; setting, 148-149; spiking, 149-150, 165-166
Dumping the ball, 76

"Feel theory" of learning, 67
Fouls, 36, 42, 43, 45, 46, 52, 128, 130, 131, 141
Free ball, 78, 109, 120
"Frier" Award (USVBA), 26, 27

Glossary of terms, 17, 179-180
Grading, 157-158, 182-186

Helm's Athletic Foundation, 24; Volleyball Hall of Fame, 24

History of volleyball (see Introduction, Friermood, 17), 66, 113, 138, 139, 143
Honor call (calling own fouls), 16, 26, 32-33, 141

International Volleyball Federation (FIVB), 23, 24, 26, 46, 85, 118, 127, 140, 141, 142

Killing the ball, 65, 76, 139
Knee pads, long sleeves, arm pads, 94, 164

"Leader in Volleyball" Award, 11, 23, 25

"Mintonette," 19

National Association of Intercollegiate Athletics (NAIA), 26
National Championships, 23, 25, 26, 27, 31, 32, 36, 39, 42, 45, 55, 63, 119, 123, 124; Amateur Athletic Union (AAU), 24, 119; National Association of Intercollegiate Athletics (NAIA), (started in 1969); National Collegiate Athletic Association (NCAA), (to start in 1970); Division for Girls' and Women's Sports (DGWS), American Association for Health, Physical Education, and Recreation, (to start in 1970); USVBA Armed Forces, 11, 24; USVBA Collegiate, 11, 23, 24, 122-123; USVBA Men's Open, 10, 21, 22, 23, 24, 32, 58, 59, 88, 117, 118, 119, 120, 121, 122; USVBA Senior Open (men over 35), 21, 24; USVBA Women's Open, 23, 24; YMCA, 20, 24
National Collegiate Athletic Association (NCAA), 19, 20, 21
Net and supports, 155-156
Net recovery shot, 96, 97, 147

Offense, definition, 179, 35, 36, 43, 47, 53, 55, 62, 63, 78, 81-82, 84, 86, 90, 91, 96, 101-111, 119, 120, 167, 168; 5-1 system, 49, 78, 83, 106-108, 139; 4-2 system, 78, 82, 104, 139, 154, 169; selection of system, 101, 106; simple 6 system, 103-104; 6-0 system, 78, 82, 83, 107-109, 139; 3-3 system, 78, 167-168
Official volleyball guides: CVA

(Canada), 35, 187; DGWS, 22, 169-170; USVBA (*see* Introduction, Friermood), 10, 11, 140

Officiating, 10, 17, 22, 27, 32, 78, 119, 127-142, 144, 155; classification of officials (DGWS), 169-170; classification of officials (USVBA), 137-140, 142, 169; linesman (*see* Diagram, 34), 119, 128, 135, 136, 137, 140, 141, 155; marks of a good official, 131, 133, 138; platform, 129, 131; referee, 45, 46, 52, 118, 127-128, 129, 130, 131, 133, 135, 136, 137, 140, 155; scorer, 25, 128, 131, 133, 135, 136, 140; signals, 131, 132, 133, 136, 138, 141; timer, 25, 128, 135, 136, 140; umpire, 128, 131, 133, 135, 137, 140, 155; uniform (USVBA), 138

Olympic Games (*see* Introduction, Friermood), 10, 11, 13, 15, 32, 45, 46, 47, 60, 103, 119, 120, 121, 122, 141, 157, 162; International Olympic Committee (IOC), 18, 20, 23, 24, 25, 26; Olympic status, 9, 23; Olympic trials, 90; U. S. Olympic Committee, 24, 26, 27, 118

Pan American Games, 10, 24, 25, 26, 27, 39, 46, 53, 57, 88, 92, 94, 103, 109, 119, 121, 122, 140, 142, 157, 162

Passing the ball, definiiton, 179, 17, 44, 45-54, 55, 57, 59, 61, 62, 77, 79, 82, 83, 85, 101, 104, 105, 120, 130, 144, 146, 147, 149, 151, 154, 163; bump pass, 43, 45, 94, 96, 98, 139, 141, 147, 155, 164, 167, 181; chest pass, 45, 141, 142; double forearm pass, definition, 179, 16, 45, 50-52, 81, 85, 96, 139, 141, 142, 147, 157, 162, 164; single forearm pass, definition, 179, 94, 95, 147; underhand pass with two hands, 45, 48-50, 128, 130, 164

Power volleyball, definition, 179, 53, 54, 66, 86, 91, 94

Psychological factors in competition, 56, 57, 62, 66, 71, 78, 86, 91, 96, 101, 103, 113, 114, 117, 118, 119, 120, 121, 122, 123

Ready position, 49, 50-53, 81, 87, 115, 119, 162, 163-164

Recreational volleyball, 9, 18, 20, 21, 103

Research in volleyball, 10, 24, 127, 157, 182

Rotation, 81, 105, 120

Rule changes, 15-16, 23, 42, 85

Rules, 24, 26, 45, 46, 107, 111, 128, 130, 131, 137, 139, 140, 141, 157, 161, 166, 169; DGWS, 16, 161, 169; FIVB, 15, 16, 104, 106, 161, 181, 187; USVBA, 16, 35, 104, 137, 138, 140, 161, 162, 169, 182

Sargent jump and reach test, 165

Scoreboard, 156

Score sheet, 25, 134, 136, 169, 170

Scouting, 81, 93

Serving area (*see* Diagram, 34)

Serving the ball, definition, 179, 35-44, 47, 77, 82, 85, 101, 105, 108, 118, 120, 130, 133, 135, 136, 139, 147, 154, 162, 164, 166, 169; hook serve, 39, 42; overhand floater serve, 35, 36-39, 53, 147; round-house serve, 35, 39; tennis serve, 38; underhand serve, 35, 36, 147

Setting the ball, definition, 179, 17, 47, 53, 55-64, 65, 69, 74, 78, 82, 83, 84, 85, 89, 90, 91, 92, 93, 98, 101, 103, 104, 105, 106, 107, 108, 109, 110, 119, 120, 130, 139, 144, 147, 150, 152, 153, 154, 155, 165, 166, 167, 168, 169; alternate setter, 108; back-line set, 62, back or over-the-head set, 60, 61, 76, 89, 105, 106, 109, 110, 151, 152; deep set, 106; double forearm set, 61; front or regular set, 61, 62, 63, 76, 90, 103, 105, 106, 151, 152; "Jap" set, 56, 61, 62, 63, 76, 103; jump set, 62, 76, 77, 109; low set, 56, 57, 61, 76, 86, 90, 103, 107, 109, 110, 152, 153; moving set, 61; one-hand set, 110; "pop" set, 61, 119; primary setter, 109; setting first ball, 63; shoot set, 56, 62, 76, 86, 90, 103, 107, 110

Skill tests, 139, 156-158; National Volleyball Skills Tournament, 23, 27

Sleep and rest, 114

Spiking line (*see* Diagram, 34)

Spiking the ball, definition, 179, 10, 44, 46, 47, 55, 56, 57, 61, 62, 65-79, 82, 83, 85, 86, 88, 89, 90, 91, 92, 93, 95, 96, 98, 101, 102, 103, 104, 105, 106, 107, 108, 109, 110, 114, 115, 116, 118, 119, 120, 130, 139, 140, 141, 144, 149, 151, 152, 153, 154, 155, 162, 165, 166, 167, 168, 169; approaches, 71-72, 149, 165-

166; "cripple" spike, 87, 89; cutting the ball, 63, 71, 74, 93; deep spike, 69, 77, 78, 92; diagonal spike, 67, 69, 71, 92, 102; dink spike, 15, 74, 76, 78, 91, 93, 103, 119, 141; down-the-line spike, 91, 93; half-speed spike, 74, 78; hitting with top spin, 66-67, 71, 75; soft spike, 78, 89, 109, 130, 141; strong-side (on-hand) spike, 72, 105, 108-109; take-offs, 69, 72, 74, 149, 165; timing, 69; weak-side (off-hand) spike, 72, 88, 108-109

Sportsmanship, 9, 13, 16, 17, 18, 26, 29, 31-33, 53

Spread of volleyball, 20

Springfield College, 9, 10, 19, 20, 21, 24, 66

"Stuffing" the ball (*see* Blocking), 87, 90, 92, 103

Substitution, 135, 136

Switching of players, 81, 84, 104, 105, 154, 169

System of plays, 101-103

Teaching techniques, 143-159

Teamwork, 47, 78, 91, 101, 109, 113, 114, 117, 118, 119, 123, 124, 166, 169

Technique player, 109

Time factor, 136

Time-out, 135, 136, 141

Tournament organization, 10, 25, 127, 133, 141

Tournaments, 57, 128

Training of players (*see* Conditioning), 17, 26, 27, 28, 57, 94, 113-125, 157

United States Volleyball Association (USVBA), (*see* Introduction, Friermood), 9, 10, 11, 15, 16, 46, 118, 119, 127, 138, 140, 142, 161, 169

Values in volleyball, 13, 17, 18, 28, 31-32, 53, 141; ethical values, 9, 13, 31, 32, 141

Verbal signals, 62, 63

Volley (*see* Passing), 65, 101

Volleyball camp, 28, 93

Wall spiking, 69, 71, 149-150

Weight training, 72, 115, 121

Women's and girls' volleyball, 6, 17, 24, 27, 40, 83, 94, 109, 117, 121, 122, 157, 161-170

World Cup Championships, 23-24, 25, 26, 27, 55, 108, 109, 114

Written tests, 137, 138, 139, 140, 156-159, 182-186

Young Men's Christian Association (YMCA), (*see* Introduction, Friermood), 9, 10, 11, 45, 106